T0001609

GREEK MYTHS

Heroes and Heroines

More classic literature available
from Macmillan Collector's Library

Greek Myths: Gods and Goddesses
edited by Jean Menzies

The Odyssey by Homer

The Iliad by Homer

The Aeneid by Virgil

GREEK MYTHS

Heroes and Heroines

Edited and introduced by
JEAN MENZIES

MACMILLAN COLLECTOR'S LIBRARY

This collection first published 2023 by Macmillan Collector's Library
an imprint of Pan Macmillan
The Smithson, 6 Briset Street, London EC1M 5NR
EU representative: Macmillan Publishers Ireland Ltd, 1st Floor,
The Liffey Trust Centre, 117–126 Sheriff Street Upper,
Dublin 1, D01 YC43
Associated companies throughout the world
www.panmacmillan.com

ISBN 978-1-5290-9336-0

1 3 5 7 9 8 6 4 2

A CIP catalogue record for this book is available from the British Library.

Casing design and endpaper pattern by Andrew Davidson
Typeset by Jouve (UK), Milton Keynes
Printed and bound in China by Imago

Visit **www.panmacmillan.com** to read more
about all our books and to buy them.

Contents

Introduction

JEAN MENZIES

If you were to recall the first legendary name that came to mind when you saw the title of this book, who would it be? If I were to hazard a guess, for many, I presume the answer would be Hercules, or Heracles as he was known by the ancient Greeks. Heracles, the semi-divine son of the lightning god Zeus and the mortal woman Alcmene. Heracles, who slayed the many-headed Hydra when no one else could. Heracles, whose strength was so impressive he could hold up the weight of the sky. Heracles, who travelled to the underworld and back, only to return with the three-headed dog Cerberus under his arm. With such feats to his name, is it any surprise we still remember him today? Some readers meanwhile might choose Achilles or Odysseus, even Jason and his stalwart crew of Argonauts. But what about Cadmus or Bellerophon? Alcestis or Atalanta? These heroes and heroines have stories too.

The heroes and heroines of Greek myth were countless and varied. It is no wonder, therefore, that some names have remained more familiar than others. The fact that we remember any at all is a testament to the continuous popularity of their stories throughout time. Whether because of their daring adventures, enchanting romances, or shocking tragedies, these heroes and heroines have captured the imagination of audiences from antiquity to today. Yet to the ancient Greeks, these men and women were more than just fodder for fascinating stories. Heroes and heroines were one step away from the gods and goddesses themselves.

According to the eighth-century-BCE Greek poet Hesiod, writing in his *Works and Days*, there were five ages of man as created by the gods and goddesses. The fourth of these ages was the age of the heroes. These men and women were the predecessors of the fifth and what became the final generation of man, our generation. Unlike ordinary men and women, this fourth race were made up of righteous warriors akin to the gods themselves. In many ways, these legendary heroes and heroines received similar veneration from ordinary ancient Greeks as did their gods and goddesses. While they were subject to death, unlike the immortal beings, the stories of these mortal heroes and heroines were far from over. From the eighth century BCE onwards, numerous long-dead heroes and heroines of myth had cults dedicated to them, where they were venerated for the virtues they demonstrated in life. But whether their parentage was semi-divine, or they were granted the favour of the gods in their lifetime, they were always and most importantly mortal, just like you or I (presumably).

Perhaps this is the reason why the stories of these men and women have remained the subject of countless retellings and reimaginations for so many centuries. From the anonymous medieval poem *Sir Orfeo*, which retells the tragic love story of Orpheus and Eurydice, to the cinematic masterpiece *Jason and the Argonauts*, which brings to life the epic sea voyage of Jason and his crew, both of which are retold again in this collection, Greek heroes and heroines have never vanished entirely from the public eye. Their stories are timeless. While the gods and goddesses of ancient Greek myth are driven by the same lust and rage that we recognize in their mortal counterparts, their immortality and power often allow them a reprieve from the consequences of their actions; any price they might pay is typically short-lived. The heroes and heroines of ancient Greece, meanwhile, suffer the cost of their choices. Their time on earth is limited and their fates are rarely their own. Is it surprising their stories remain so relatable?

The fifteen stories brought together in this volume were written between the Victorian and Edwardian eras by twelve authors who were as enthralled by the enduring narratives of these ancient heroes and heroines as any other generation. Each time a myth is retold, traces of the period and culture in which it was composed shine through, and this is equally true for this collection. The nineteenth and early twentieth centuries witnessed major political, religious, and social reform in the countries from which these writers hailed. The excitement of innovation and desire to reclaim tradition simultaneously had a hold on society. Yet whether the authors compiled here wrote their versions for children, as Blanche Winder and Nathaniel Hawthorne did, or for adults like Jean Lang and Carl Witt, their work straddled both of these worlds. They took ancient tales of heroes and heroines and told them anew for audiences two millennia removed from the original myths. For consistency, Latin names have been changed to their original Greek in this collection.

I like to think both the range and the timelessness of themes in these myths are also present in this collection. Within these pages you will find tales of love both doomed and joyful; face the consequences of arrogance and greed; cringe at reckless actions while marvelling as cunning plans unfold. You will witness the bravery and strength of heroes and heroines alike, as they slay monstrous beasts and outwit scheming foes. Some myths will end happily while some will not, and others you will have to make your own mind up about. There will be names you will recognize, like Heracles and Circe, and many more I suspect you might not, like Ceyx and Halcyone. And, by the end, you will hopefully have a better understanding of why these heroes and heroines meant so much to the ancient Greeks who worshipped them, how their stories continued to capture the imaginations of nineteenth- and twentieth-century audiences, and what value they might offer modern readers, whether for entertainment or education's sake.

GREEK MYTHS

Heroes and Heroines

THE KING WITH
THE TOUCH OF GOLD

The myth of King Midas is one that, since antiquity, has taken on a life of its own. Many modern readers I am sure, although familiar with the bare bones of Midas's story, might not even have known that he's a figure from Greek mythology. The king whose touch can turn anything to gold has become a cultural icon not least for the timeless message his story denotes: greed is bad. When Midas is presented with the opportunity to benefit from the god Dionysus's gratitude after helping his friend, he goes too far and asks for the ability to turn anything and everything into gold. As you might be able to predict, this gift is not what Midas hopes it would be. The moral in this story has appealed to countless generations, as Blanche Winder's retelling makes clear, but does Midas learn his lesson? You will have to read on to see.

Dionysus, of whom you heard in another story, was very powerful and clever, and could give to human beings almost any gift for which they asked. No wonder the helmsman was pleased to be under his protection! However, Dionysus had a good deal of mischief in his nature, and here is a tale of a prank he once played upon a rich and greedy King.

The King's name was Midas. He was very wealthy indeed, but he was a shocking miser. He loved gold for its own sake; not for what he could do with it. He collected as much of it as he could, and he loved to count his coins by the hour together. Some of the treasures in his palace were made of pure gold, and he was never tired of looking at them, and handling them, and wishing from his heart that he owned many more.

One morning King Midas was sitting on his throne, when there was a great noise outside, and in came a number of his harvesters and gardeners, leading a strange figure tied up with chains of roses! It was old Silenus, who had lost himself— and not only himself, but all his friends and his prancing wild ass as well. He was very miserable and upset, for the country people had found him asleep in the King's rose-garden, and thought it a great thing to have caught a wild Satyr. Midas was delighted, for some of his own distant relations were Satyrs; and he entertained Silenus most hospitably for ten days. Then he said he would himself take him back to Dionysus, and he set off through the woods in search of the vine-crowned Immortal. When they reached the flowery glade where Dionysus was living just then, King Midas gave Silenus into the care of his pupil, and prepared to set off home again.

But Dionysus stopped him and said that the King, in return for his kindness, might ask for any gift that he wanted. Midas instantly declared that what he wanted, above everything else, was more money and more treasure. Would Dionysus grant him the gift of turning everything he touched into gold?

Dionysus smiled, and made a little movement of warning with his head. Then he told Midas he would grant his request. But the Shining Immortal shook his head again, and looked amused, as the King went joyfully away. Dionysus was wondering how long it would be before Midas felt very sorry indeed that such a gift had been presented to him.

The greedy King walked homewards through the woods, much pleased with his morning's work. Presently he thought he would put his wonderful new power to the test. Lifting his hand, endowed with its strange magic, to a green bough that hung just overhead, he drew down a twig, his eyes, shining with excitement, fixed upon the pretty brown bark and green leaves. Lo! and behold, the moment his fingers touched the twig it turned into the brightest, purest gold, and, breaking it away from the branch, Midas carried it homewards with him, his heart beating with excitement as he turned it this way and that, to make it glitter and flash in the sun.

On went the King, holding aloft his golden twig. Presently he thought he would try his power again, so he stooped and picked up a stone; this also turned immediately into gold. Putting it into the pocket of his robe—which had itself been quietly turning into gold all this time—he walked a little farther and came out of the wood into a field of corn. He gathered one of the ears, and that, too, shone instantly with a golden radiance in his fingers. Then he reached his own orchard and, plucking an apple, found himself laden with another treasure. The same thing happened when he picked a bunch of roses in the garden. So, laden with golden fruit and corn and flowers, his pockets heavy with golden stones, and his golden robes trailing heavily about him, King Midas walked up the steps of his palace, and, passing through his surprised courtiers, reached the steps of his throne. He paused for a moment, laid down his spoils, and placed his hand on a pillar—which, of course, turned into gold on the spot. Then he told his lords-in-waiting to send out invitations for a great feast to be held in the banqueting-hall as soon as ever the tables could be spread with delicious food and wine. "For," thought he, "I will show off my magical gift to all the neighbouring princes and their ministers! How they will envy me my extraordinary powers!"

King Midas sat and played with his glittering golden treasures until the feast was spread, and the guests had gathered round the table. Then he walked, very slowly and magnificently, to his place at the head. Everybody was watching him, for they had heard all sorts of rumours, and were very excited to see what would happen.

King Midas took his seat, and requested his visitors to start eating and drinking. They at once began to enjoy the savoury dishes, the delicate fruits, and the rich cakes. The King watched them for a moment, then, with a smile, lifted a crystal goblet, full of water mixed with wine, to his own lips. He wanted to enjoy their surprise when the goblet turned to gold.

And turn to gold it did—but the water and the wine turned with it! No sooner had the fragrant purple liquid touched the royal lips than down it trickled in a golden stream over the King's chin! Thirsty and dismayed, he set down the goblet, and reached for some bread, only to find that it turned into gold before he could swallow it! So with the fruit—so with the cakes—so with the savoury meat-pies! The guests, whispering among themselves, began to smile behind their damask table-napkins; and at last King Midas, hungry, thirsty, and very angry, rose from the feast and hurried away.

But a worse trouble even than hunger and thirst was in store for him. Coming to meet him, across the hall of the palace, were his beautiful little sons and daughters, radiant with health, and laughing over their play. They ran to him to kiss him, and, unthinkingly, he took one of them into his arms: to his intense horror, he found that the child in his embrace changed into a golden statue!

He set the statue down, and burst into tears of agony. Then, waving away the other startled and dismayed children, he went to weep in his own chamber. After a night of despair upon a hard, golden bed, he rose early and went off through the orchards and cornfields, until he reached the wood where Dionysus lived. Hurrying down the green, shadowy glades, he never paused until he found the vine-crowned Immortal, seated among his goat-footed friends, with all his wild beasts round him.

Falling on his knees, King Midas lifted imploring hands, and sobbed out his trouble, begging Dionysus to take his terrible gift away from him. So Dionysus told the King he must go and wash at the source of a river not very far away, and he would become quite ordinary once more. The poor King hardly waited to say "thank you" before he hurried off, never stopping until he reached the source of the river, where it bubbled, clear and cool, from the rock. He sprang straight into the water, and plunged his head below the ripples. Behold! to his joy the sticky gold was all washed from his mouth and the sparkling fragments from his wet hair. When he climbed the bank again, he knew that he was, once more, like other men.

But a strange thing had happened! The spell that Dionysus had laid on Midas could never be destroyed, so instead of remaining with the King, it passed into the river itself! A new glimmer shone ever after through the water—the sands ran yellow—and the flowers on the banks nodded golden heads, and dropped golden petals on to golden grass. Even the corn that was sown in the fields near by would sometimes sprout golden ears, and the ground was always hard and difficult to plough. But King Midas was only too happy when, on reaching home, he found that the spell was removed, and that he had his child again, instead of the poor little gold statue that he had left glittering among the pillars of the hall.

King Midas was quite cured of his miserliness, but he seemed to be born to trouble, and he had another unhappy adventure in his old age. He had always been fond of wandering in the woods, and he was a very great admirer of Pan and his music. One day he found Pan and Apollo quarrelling in a quiet, green glade as to which could make the sweeter melody, Pan with his pipes or Apollo with his lyre. The nymphs, who sat round listening, seemed quite unable to judge, so both Pan and Apollo appealed to Midas to settle the dispute. The King, without a moment's hesitation, declared that Pan's music was the more delightful—whereupon Apollo lost his temper and cried angrily:

"Whoever says a thing like that must have ass's ears!"

No sooner had he spoken than the unhappy King's ears turned into the ears of an ass, just as quickly as his apples and bread had turned into gold!

Poor King Midas! He went home in no lordly manner this time, but as quickly and quietly as he could, and, sending for his lord-of-the-bed-chamber, at once ordered an enormous new head-dress. Until it came, he hid from sight. With the great new head-dress on his head nobody could see the ears, and he only looked like a rather eccentric King of the East. However, he was not able to keep the secret from his barber, whom the King threatened with immediate death if he ever told. The barber was so worried by the knowledge that he felt quite sure he would, one day, let it out. In order to relieve his feelings, he used, each time he cut King Midas's hair, to go down to the river, and put his face deep among the reeds. Then he would whisper:

"King Midas has ass's ears! King Midas has ass's ears! King Midas has ass's ears!"

Over and over again he would whisper it, until his mind felt relieved, when he would go home again in peace. But unfortunately the reeds learnt the words by heart, and began to repeat them, so that anyone who passed near the river at twilight would hear a little whisper:

"King Midas has ass's ears!"

This happened so often that at last the secret was a secret no longer. But, as it was only the reeds who told it, nobody took much notice, and King Midas lived quite happily, dressed up in his big cap. No doubt, though, as he grew still older, he gave up wandering in the woods, for nobody could tell what would happen to any mortal who made friends with strange beings like Dionysus and Pan.

CADMUS AND EUROPA

Cadmus is one of the lesser-talked-about heroes of Greek mythology, yet the role he played in ancient myth was significant. In many ways, in fact, he was the first hero of Greek mythology. His journey begins when he sets out across the sea to rescue his sister Europa, who was abducted by the god Zeus in the form of a bull. He travels from Asia to Europe only to abandon his original mission in favour of founding the Greek city of Thebes. Of course, he meets with a number of obstacles along his journey and, while he is off adventuring across an unfamiliar continent, he seemingly forgets all about Europa. You will not, therefore, learn the fate of this hero's sister in James Baldwin's account, so for those who are curious, Zeus takes Europa to Crete where she marries the king, Asterius, and becomes queen.

I. THE BULL

In Asia there lived a king who had two children, a boy and a girl. The boy's name was Cadmus, and the girl's name was Europa. The king's country was a very small one. He could stand on his house top and see the whole of it. On one side of it there were mountains, and on the other side was the sea. The king thought that it was the center of the world, and he did not know much about other lands and people.

Yet he was very happy in his own little kingdom, and very fond of his children. And he had good reason to be proud of them; for Cadmus grew up to be the bravest young man in the land, and Europa to be the fairest maiden that had ever been seen. But sad days came to them all at last.

One morning Europa went out into a field near the seashore to pick flowers. Her father's cattle were in the field, grazing among the sweet clover. They were all very tame, and Europa knew every one of them by name. The herdsman was lying in the shade under a tree, trying to make music on a little flute of straw. Europa had played in the field a thousand times before, and no one had ever thought of any harm befalling her.

That morning she noticed that there was a strange bull with the herd. He was very large and as white as snow; and he had soft brown eyes which somehow made him look very gentle and kind. At first he did not even look at Europa, but went here and there, eating the tender grass which grew among the clover. But when she had gathered her apron full of daisies and buttercups, he came slowly towards her. She was not at all afraid of him; and so she stopped to look at him, he was so handsome. He came close to her, and rubbed her arm with his nose to say "Good-morning!"

She stroked his head and neck, and he seemed much pleased. Then she made a wreath of daisies, and hung it round his neck. He looked at her with his soft kind eyes, and seemed to thank her; and in a little while, he lay down among the clover. Europa then made a smaller wreath, and climbed upon his back to twine it round his horns. But all at once he sprang up, and ran away so swiftly that Europa could not help herself. She did not dare to jump off while he was going so fast, and all that she could think to do was to hold fast to his neck and scream very loud.

The herdsman under the tree heard her scream, and jumped up to see what was the matter. He saw the bull running with her towards the shore. He ran after them as fast as he could, but it was of no use. The bull leaped into the sea, and swam swiftly away, with poor Europa on his back. Several other people had seen him, and now they ran to tell the king. Soon the whole town was alarmed. Everybody ran out to the shore and looked. All that could be seen was something white moving very fast over the calm, blue water; and soon it was out of sight.

The king sent out his fastest ship to try to overtake the bull. The sailors rowed far out to sea, much farther than any ship had ever gone before; but no trace of Europa could be found. When they came back, everybody felt that there was no more hope. All the women and children in the town wept for the lost Europa. The king shut himself up in his house, and did not eat nor drink for three days. Then he called his son Cadmus, and bade him take a ship and go in search of his sister; and he told him that, no matter what dangers might be in his way, he must not come back until she was found.

Cadmus was glad to go. He chose twenty brave young men to go with him, and set sail the very next day. It was a great undertaking; for they were to pass through an unknown sea, and they did not know what lands they would come to. Indeed, it was feared that they would never come to any land at all. Ships did not dare to go far from the shore in those days. But Cadmus and his friends were not afraid. They were ready to face any danger.

In a few days they came to a large island called Cyprus. Cadmus went on shore, and tried to talk with the strange people who lived there. They were very kind to him, but they did not understand his language. At last he made out by signs to tell them who he was, and to ask them if they had seen his little sister Europa or the white bull that had carried her away. They shook their heads and pointed to the west.

Then the young men sailed on in their little ship. They came to many islands, and stopped at every one, to see if they could find any trace of Europa; but they heard no news of her at all. At last, they came to the country which we now call Greece. It was a new country then, and only a few people lived there, and Cadmus soon learned to speak their language well. For a long time he wandered from one little town to another, always telling the story of his lost sister.

One day an old man told Cadmus that if he would go to Delphi and ask the Pythia, perhaps she could tell him all about Europa. Cadmus had never heard of Delphi or of the Pythia, and he asked the old man what he meant.

"I will tell you," said the man. "Delphi is a town, built near the foot of Mount Parnassus, at the very center of the earth. It is the town of Apollo, the Bringer of Light; and there is a temple there, built close to the spot where Apollo killed a black serpent, many, many years ago. The temple is the most wonderful place in the world. In the middle of the floor there is a wide crack, or crevice; and this crevice goes down, down into the rock, nobody knows how deep. A strange odor comes up out of the crevice; and if any one breathes much of it, he is apt to fall over and lose his senses."

"But who is the Pythia that you spoke about?" asked Cadmus.

"I will tell you," said the old man. "The Pythia is a wise woman, who lives in the temple. When anybody asks her a hard question, she takes a three-legged stool, called a tripod, and sets it over the crevice in the floor. Then she sits on the stool and breathes the strange odor; and instead of losing her senses as other people would do, she talks with Apollo; and Apollo tells her how to answer the question. Men from all parts of the world go there to ask about things which they would like to know. The temple is full of the beautiful and costly gifts which they have brought for the Pythia. Sometimes she answers them plainly, and sometimes she answers them in riddles; but what she says always comes true."

So Cadmus went to Delphi to ask the Pythia about his lost sister. The wise woman was very kind to him; and when he had given her a beautiful golden cup to pay her for her trouble, she sat down on the tripod and breathed the strange odor which came up through the crevice in the rock. Then her face grew pale, and her eyes looked wild, and she seemed to be in great pain; but they said that she was talking with Apollo. Cadmus asked her to tell him what had become of Europa. She said that Zeus, in the form of a white bull, had carried her away, and that it would be of no use to look for her any more.

"But what shall I do?" said Cadmus. "My father told me not to turn back till I should find her."

"Your father is dead," said the Pythia, "and a strange king rules in his place. You must stay in Greece, for there is work here for you to do."

"What must I do?" said Cadmus.

"Follow the white cow," said the Pythia; "and on the hill where she lies down, you must build a city."

Cadmus did not understand what she meant by this; but she would not speak another word.

"This must be one of her riddles," he said, and he left the temple.

III. THE DRAGON

When Cadmus went out of the temple, he saw a snow-white cow standing not far from the door. She seemed to be waiting for him, for she looked at him with her large brown eyes, and then turned and walked away. Cadmus thought of what the Pythia had just told him, and so he followed her. All day and all night he walked through a strange wild country where no one lived; and two of the young men who had sailed with Cadmus from his old home were with him.

When the sun rose the next morning, they saw that they were on the top of a beautiful hill, with woods on one side and a grassy meadow on the other. There the cow lay down.

"Here we will build our city," said Cadmus.

Then the young men made a fire of dry sticks, and Cadmus killed the cow. They thought that if they should burn some of her flesh, the smell of it would go up to the sky and be pleasing to Zeus and the Mighty Folk who lived with him among the clouds; and in this way they hoped to make friends with Zeus so that he would not hinder them in their work.

But they needed water to wash the flesh and their hands; and so one of the young men went down the hill to find some. He was gone so long that the other young man became uneasy and went after him.

Cadmus waited for them till the fire had burned low. He waited and waited till the sun was high in the sky. He called and shouted, but no one answered him. At last he took his sword in his hand and went down to see what was the matter.

He followed the path which his friends had taken, and soon came to a fine stream of cold water at the foot of a hill. He saw something move among the bushes which grew near it. It was a fierce dragon, waiting to spring upon him. There was blood on the grass and leaves, and it was not hard to guess what had become of the two young men.

The beast sprang at Cadmus, and tried to seize him with its sharp claws. But Cadmus leaped quickly aside and struck it in the neck with his long sword. A great stream of black blood gushed out, and the dragon soon fell to the ground dead. Cadmus had seen many fearful sights, but never anything so dreadful as this beast. He had never been in so great danger before. He sat down on the ground and trembled; and, all the time, he was weeping for his two friends. How now was he to build a city, with no one to help him?

IV. THE CITY

While Cadmus was still weeping he was surprised to hear some one calling him. He stood up and looked around. On the hillside before him was a tall woman who had a helmet on her head and a shield in her hand. Her eyes were gray, and her face, though not beautiful, was very noble. Cadmus knew at once that she was Athena, the queen of the air—she who gives wisdom to men.

Athena told Cadmus that he must take out the teeth of the dragon and sow them in the ground. He thought that would be a queer kind of seed. But she said that if he would do this, he would soon have men enough to help him build his city; and, before he could say a word, she had gone out of his sight.

The dragon had a great many teeth—so many that when Cadmus had taken them out they filled his helmet heaping full. The next thing was to find a good place to sow them. Just as he turned away from the stream, he saw a yoke of oxen standing a little way off. He went to them and found that they were hitched to a plow. What more could he want? The ground in the meadow was soft and black, and he drove the plow up and down, making long furrows as he went. Then he dropped the teeth, one by one, into the furrows and covered them over with the rich soil. When he had sown all of them in this way, he sat down on the hillside and watched to see what would happen.

In a little while the soil in the furrows began to stir. Then, at every place that a tooth had been dropped, something bright grew up. It was a brass helmet. The helmets pushed their way up, and soon the faces of men were seen underneath, then their shoulders, then their arms, then their bodies; and then, before Cadmus could think, a thousand warriors leaped out of the furrows and shook off the black earth which was clinging to them. Every man was clothed in a suit of brass armor; and every one had a long spear in his right hand and a shield in his left.

Cadmus was frightened when he saw the strange crop which had grown up from the dragon's teeth. The men looked so fierce that he feared they would kill him if they saw him. He hid himself behind his plow and then began to throw stones at them. The warriors did not know where the stones came from, but each thought that his neighbor had struck him. Soon they began to fight among themselves. Man after man was killed, and in a little while only five were left alive. Then Cadmus ran towards them and called out:

"Hold! Stop fighting! You are my men, and must come with me. We will build a city here."

The men obeyed him. They followed Cadmus to the top of the hill; and they were such good workmen that in a few days they had built a house on the spot where the cow had lain down.

After that they built other houses, and people came to live in them. They called the town Cadmeia, after Cadmus who was its first king. But when the place had grown to be a large city, it was known by the name of Thebes.

Cadmus was a wise king. The Mighty Folk who lived with Zeus amid the clouds were well pleased with him and helped him in more ways than one. After a while he married Harmonia, the beautiful daughter of Mars. All the Mighty Ones were at the wedding; and Athena gave the bride a wonderful necklace about which you may learn something more at another time.

But the greatest thing that Cadmus did is yet to

be told. He was the first schoolmaster of the Greeks, and taught them the letters which were used in his own country across the sea. They called the first of these letters *alpha* and the second *beta*, and that is why men speak of the *alphabet* to this day. And when the Greeks had learned the alphabet from Cadmus, they soon began to read and write, and to make beautiful and useful books.

As for the maiden Europa, she was carried safe over the sea to a distant shore. She may have been happy in the new, strange land to which she was taken—I cannot tell; but she never heard of friends or home again. Whether it was really Zeus in the form of a bull that carried her away, nobody knows. It all happened so long ago that there may have been some mistake about the story; and I should not think it strange if it were a sea robber who stole her from her home, and a swift ship with white sails that bore her away. Of one thing I am very sure: she was loved so well by all who knew her that the great unknown country to which she was taken has been called after her name ever since—Europe.

BELLEROPHON

Bellerophon is another underrepresented hero in twentieth- and twenty-first-century popular culture. In fact, one of his most well-known accomplishments has become commonly associated with Heracles instead: the taming and befriending of the flying horse Pegasus. Bellerophon is a name any mythology enthusiast should learn, however, as his achievements were many and varied. As Carl Witt narrates, the hero went from living in exile to marrying a princess of Lycia during his lifetime. He was also one of the heroes blessed by the goddess Athena, who was often seen assisting him in his adventures. Not included in this version, however, is his eventual fall from grace. When the hero demands he should join the gods on Olympus for his deeds, the gods are not impressed. Zeus grants his wish, but only to make him a pack mule for his thunderbolts. No hero is immune from the whims of the gods, it seems.

In the city of Corinth there were two young brothers, the sons of Glaucus, the son of Sisyphus, one of whom was called Bellerophon, and was gifted by the gods with great strength and beauty. But one day, when he was out hunting with his brother, he threw his spear at a hind, and the spear missed its aim and accidentally hit his brother, who died of the wound. Bellerophon was very much grieved, and wished he could have been killed himself rather than have done this; but nevertheless he had to leave his father's house and the city of Corinth, for everyone who killed another by accident was banished. He set out, not knowing who would receive him, but he determined first of all to seek for someone who would purge him from the stain of blood; for the Greeks held that whoever had killed another, even though unintentionally, was defiled, and needed to be purified by means of sacrifices and baths. It was not everyone who understood how to do this, but Bellerophon heard that King Proetus was learned in these matters, and he went to him and begged him to purify him.

Proetus did what was necessary, and as the young hero pleased him, he begged him to stay with him and be his guest, and treated him as his own son. But the queen was so much struck with the beauty of Bellerophon that she longed to have him for her husband, and she had a secret conversation with him, and proposed that they should both flee out of the country and be married. But Bellerophon could not have acted so ungratefully towards his kind host if the queen had been the most beautiful woman in the world, and he told her plainly that he would not do as she wished. Then all her fondness was turned into hatred and a fierce desire to kill him, and she went to her husband and said that Bellerophon had begged her to go away with him and be his wife, and that when she had refused, he had got angry and had said he should put the king to death. The king believed his wife and was exceedingly angry, but as Bellerophon was his guest, he would not himself lay hands on him. He thought of another way of taking his life, and concealing his resentment, asked Bellerophon if he would take a message from him to his father-in-law Iobates, who was king of Lycia. It was a long distance by sea as well as by land to the country of Lycia, but Bellerophon was glad to do anything to please Proetus, and he at once promised to go.

Proetus took a wooden tablet, and made signs upon it to signify that his father-in-law was to put the messenger to death, and then he covered the tablet with another, and tied a string round it. This was the way in which all letters were sent at that time, for paper and ink were not yet invented.

Bellerophon took the letter and set out, suspecting nothing. He travelled for some time till he came to the sea, where he found a ship about to sail to the opposite coast, so he got into it, and after a few days' journey, arrived at the country of King Iobates who received him in a very friendly manner. It was not then the custom to ask a guest his name and his business as soon as he arrived, and for nine days Iobates entertained Bellerophon without knowing who he was, and every day he sacrificed a bull, and feasted with his guest. The Greeks used to cut off the thigh-bones of the animals they sacrificed, for the gods; they covered these bones with skin and placed them in the fire to make a pleasant odour for them, and then they consumed the rest of the animal themselves. On the tenth day, King Iobates asked his guest what his name was and whether he had brought any message, and Bellerophon told his name and delivered the letter which Proetus had sent. But when the king had made out the meaning of the signs, he was horrified, for he had become very fond of the young hero, and the idea of killing him had been far from his thoughts. Still, as his son-in-law urged him to do this, he supposed that Bellerophon must have committed some great crime, and he determined to carry out the wishes of Proetus. He might have murdered Bellerophon in his sleep, but he would not do that,—he willed rather that he should die like a hero, fighting for his life. There was at that time in the land of Lycia a horrible monster called the Chimaera, whose forepart was like a lion, her back like a dragon, and in the middle she was a goat. At night the Chimaera remained on her mountain, but in the daytime she came down and laid waste the cornfields and devoured men and cattle, causing great distress all over the country. The king asked Bellerophon whether he had courage enough to encounter the monster, and Bellerophon said yes, for he longed to be a real hero whose exploits men relate in song, and he was ready to venture upon any errand however dangerous it might be. So he armed himself with spear and sword, and set out in search of the Chimaera.

The gods were pleased with him for his courage, but they knew that he must perish in the fight if they did not help him. He had not gone far when there came down from heaven a beautiful horse with wings like a bird, which flew round and round him. This horse was called Pegasus, and belonged to the gods. Bellerophon was delighted with the beautiful animal, and tried to attract him by whistling and coaxing. At last he persuaded him to come near enough to be stroked, and after that the hero soon succeeded in placing himself on his back, and they flew away together through the air. Bellerophon was the first man who had ever ridden upon such a horse. He would have found Pegasus a perfect steed if he had understood what was said to him, but instead of doing as he wished, he always went the wrong way. So he dismounted and continued his journey on foot, and Pegasus flew round him in beautiful curves, and was his travelling companion. By-and-by he met an old man who was a soothsayer, and he asked the hero how he came to possess such a beautiful animal. Bellerophon told him all about it, and added that he wished he knew how to make the horse obedient to his will, and then the soothsayer said that he would soon come to a place dedicated to the goddess Athene, and that if anyone who was in need of counsel chose to sleep in the temple, the goddess would often help him by a dream. Bellerophon resolved to try this, and as the stars were beginning to shine, he reached the temple of Athene; and he went in and stretched himself on the floor with his head resting on the step of the altar for a pillow, while the horse slept outside the door. When it was nearly morning, the goddess Athene appeared to him in a dream and told him that she loved all brave heroes, and was glad to help him. She showed him a golden ribbon, and said that if he put it into the mouth of the horse and held the two ends in his hand, it would be a means of communication between them. She placed the golden ribbon in his hand, and he awoke, still holding it. It was the first bridle, and had been invented by the goddess Athene. He went out at once, put the ribbon into the mouth of the horse, and swung himself on to his back. Then they flew away, and the steed obeyed the rein, and went just where the hero wished. Bellerophon was very much pleased at this, and he offered up prayers and thanks to Athene for the help she had given him.

After this Bellerophon continued his journey through the air, and when it was evening he came to a mountain by the sea from which he saw a flame of fire ascending, and this showed him where the Chimaera was. He flew towards the place on the back of Pegasus, and perceived the horrible form of the monster. Pegasus hovered over her, and Bellerophon shot an arrow which wounded her in the neck and gave her great pain; this made her furious, and she stood up on her hind feet and puffed out her fiery breath into the air, hoping to scorch Bellerophon to death, but he was so high up that he was not hurt by it; and he shot her in the back with another arrow, so that she rolled about in pain, howling horribly, and then he sent a third arrow into her side. She had now only strength enough to moan, and in a little while she was dead. Then Bellerophon could come down to the mountain which was no longer unsafe for people to set foot upon; he slept there that night, and in the morning he cut off the head of the Chimaera, and set out upon his way home again.

When Bellerophon stood before Iobates with the head of the Chimaera in his hand, the king was very much astonished, for he had thought there was not a chance that he would escape being killed by her. But he was still desirous of carrying out the wishes of Proetus, and he therefore sent the hero to fight against a barbarous people on the outskirts of his kingdom, who lived by plunder and robbery. No one who had hitherto been sent against them had ever returned alive, but the gods helped Bellerophon, and he slew a great many of the robbers and drove away the rest.

A third time the king sent him away, and now it was to fight against a still stronger people. But after a few days had passed, there came messengers to tell him that the hero had put the enemy to flight and was about to return. Then the king chose out the strongest Lycian youths, and set them in ambush on the road leading to the city. In the evening, however, Bellerophon entered the palace unhurt. The king thought he must have come by another road, and he asked him if he had met nothing on the way. Bellerophon answered, 'Near the city there were some cowardly knaves lying in ambush, whom I slew.' Then the king knew that Bellerophon must be under the protection of the gods, and he laid aside all thoughts of doing him any injury, and told him that on account of the request of Proetus he had sent him on these expeditions in order that he might meet his death, but that from henceforth he would be his friend. He gave him the most beautiful of all his daughters for his wife, and begged him to stay with him and take part in the government of the country. The wedding soon took place, and from that time Bellerophon had a kingly staff like Iobates, and sat beside him on the throne to give judgment in all cases of difficulty. The Lycians gave him some of their land for his own, of which one part consisted of corn-fields, another part was a wine country, and the third was planted with beautiful fruit trees. The winged horse Pegasus was well taken care of, and Bellerophon ever treasured him as one of his dearest friends.

PERSEUS

Perseus's conception must be one of the strangest in Greek myth, which is saying something indeed, for there are numerous contenders. While in captivity, Danae, Perseus's mother, is visited by Zeus in the form a shower of gold, which even our author cannot explain. During this visit she becomes pregnant with Zeus's son, Perseus. From such extraordinary beginnings Perseus's tale was sure to be an impressive one. Most famous, however, is probably his defeat of the gorgon Medusa, who could turn any man to stone simply by catching his gaze. In some accounts, Medusa's tale is an especially tragic one; she was turned into a gorgon by Athena after being sexually assaulted by Poseidon. The details of her story are not included in Andrew Lang's account, which is focused on the greatness of Perseus. Take note, however, that there are often more stories that lie behind the myths we read.

I. THE PRISON OF DANAE

Many years before the Siege of Troy there lived in Greece two princes who were brothers and deadly enemies. Each of them wished to be king both of Argos (where Diomede ruled in the time of the Trojan war), and of Tiryns. After long wars one of the brothers, Proetus, took Tiryns, and built the great walls of huge stones, and the palace; while the other brother, Acrisius, took Argos, and he married Eurydice, a princess of the Royal House of Lacedæmon, where Menelaus and Helen were King and Queen in later times.

Acrisius had one daughter, Danae, who became the most beautiful woman in Greece, but he had no son. This made him very unhappy, for he thought that, when he grew old, the sons of his brother Proetus would attack him, and take his lands and city, if he had no son to lead his army. His best plan would have been to find some brave young prince, like Theseus, and give Danae to him for his wife, and their sons would be leaders of the men of Argos. But Acrisius preferred to go to the prophetic maiden of the temple of Apollo at Delphi (or Pytho, as it was then called), and ask what chance he had of being the father of a son.

The maiden seldom had good news to give any man; but at least this time it was easy to understand what she said. She went down into the deep cavern below the temple floor, where it was said that a strange mist or steam flowed up out of the earth, and made her fall into a strange sleep, in which she could walk and speak, but knew not what she was singing, for she sang her prophecies. At last she came back, very pale, with her laurel wreath twisted awry, and her eyes open, but seeing nothing. She sang that Acrisius would never have a son; but that his daughter would bear a son, who would kill him.

Acrisius mounted his chariot, sad and sorry, and was driven homewards. On the way he never spoke a word, but was thinking how he might escape from the prophecy, and baffle the will of Zeus, the chief of the gods. He did not know that Zeus himself had looked down upon Danae and fallen in love with her, nor did Danae know.

The only sure way to avoid the prophecy was to kill Danae, and Acrisius thought of doing this; but he loved her too much; and he was afraid that his people would rise against him, if he slew his daughter, the pride of their hearts. Still another fear was upon Acrisius, which will be explained later in the story. He could think of nothing better than to build a house all of bronze, in the court of his palace, a house sunk deep in the earth, but with part of the roof open to the sky, as was the way in all houses then; the light came in from above, and the smoke of the fire went out in the same way. This chamber Acrisius built, and in it he shut up poor Danae with the woman that had been her nurse. They saw nothing, hills or plains or sea, men or trees, they only saw the sun at midday, and the sky, and the free birds flitting across it. There Danae lay, and was weary and sad, and she could not guess why her father thus imprisoned her. He used to visit her often and seemed kind and sorry for her, but he would never listen when she implored him to sell her for a slave into a far country, so that, at least, she might see the world in which she lived.

Now one day a mysterious thing happened; the old poet Pindar, who lived long after, in the time of the war between the Greeks and the King of Persia, says that a living stream of gold flowed down from the sky and filled the chamber of Danae. Some time after this Danae bore a baby, a son, the strongest and most beautiful of children. She and her nurse kept it secret, and the child was brought up in an inner chamber of the house of bronze. It was difficult to prevent so lively a child from making a noise in his play, and one day, when Acrisius was with Danae, the boy, now three or four years old, escaped from his nurse, and ran from her room, laughing and shouting. Acrisius rushed out, and saw the nurse catch the child, and throw her mantle over him. Acrisius seized the boy, who stood firm on his little legs, with his head high, frowning at his grandfather, and gazing in anger out of his large blue eyes. Acrisius saw that this child would be dangerous when he became a man, and in great anger he bade his guards take the nurse out, and strangle her with a rope, while Danae knelt weeping at his feet.

When they were alone he said to Danae: 'Who is the father of this child?' but she, with her boy on her arm, slipped past Acrisius, and out of the open door, and up the staircase, into the open air. She ran to the altar of Zeus, which was built in the court, and threw her arms round it, thinking that there no man dared to touch her. 'I cry to Zeus that is throned in the highest, the Lord of Thunder,' she said: 'for he and no other is the father of my boy, even Perseus.' The sky was bright and blue without a cloud, and Danae cried in vain. There came no flash of lightning nor roll of thunder.

'Is it even so?' said Acrisius, 'then let Zeus

guard his own.' He bade his men drag Danae from the altar; and lock her again in the house of bronze; while he had a great strong chest made. In that chest he had the cruelty to place Danae and her boy, and he sent them out to sea in a ship, the sailors having orders to let the chest down into the waters when they were far from shore. They dared not disobey, but they put food and a skin of wine, and two skins of water in the chest, and lowered it into the sea, which was perfectly calm and still. It was their hope that some ship would come sailing by, perhaps a ship of Phœnician merchant-men, who would certainly save Danae and the child, if only that they might sell them for slaves.

King Acrisius himself was not ignorant that this might happen, and that his grandson might live to be the cause of his death. But the Greeks believed that if any man killed one of his own kinsfolk, he would be pursued and driven mad by the Furies called the Erinyes, terrible winged women with cruel claws. These winged women drove Orestes, the son of Agamemnon, fleeing like a madman through the world, because he slew his own mother, Clytaemnestra, to avenge his father, whom she and Ægisthus had slain. Nothing was so much dreaded as these Furies, and therefore Acrisius did not dare to slay his daughter and his grandson,

Perseus, but only put them in the way of being drowned. He heard no more of them, and hoped that both of their bodies were rolling in the waves, or that their bones lay bleaching on some unknown shore. But he could not be certain—indeed, he soon knew better—and as long as he lived, he lived in fear that Perseus had escaped, and would come and slay him, as the prophetess had said in her song.

The chest floated on the still waters, and the sea birds swooped down to look at it, and passed by, with one waft of their wings. The sun set, and Danae watched the stars, the Bear and Orion with his belt, and wrapped her boy up warm, and he slept sound, for he never knew fear, in his mother's arms. The Dawn came in her golden throne, and Danae saw around her the blue sharp crests of the mountains of the islands that lay scattered like water lilies on the seas of Greece. If only the current would drift her to an island, she thought, and prayed in her heart to the Gods of Good Help, Pallas Athênê, and Hermes of the Golden Wand. Soon she began to hope that the chest was drawing near an island. She turned her head in the opposite direction for a long while, and then looked forward again. She was much nearer the island, and could see the smoke going up from cottages among the trees. But she drifted on and drifted past the end of the isle, and on with the current, and so all day.

A weary day she had, for the boy was full of play, and was like to capsize the chest. She gave him some wine and water, and presently he fell asleep, and Danae watched the sea and the distant isles till night came again. It was dark, with no moon, and the darker because the chest floated into the shadow of a mountain, and the current drew it near the shore. But Danae dared not hope again; men would not be abroad, she thought, in the night. As she lay thus helpless, she saw a light moving on the sea, and she cried as loud as she could cry. Then the light stopped, and a man's shout came to her over the water, and the light moved swiftly towards her. It came from a brazier set on a pole in a boat, and now Danae could see the bright sparks that shone in the drops from the oars, for the boat was being rowed towards her, as fast as two strong men could pull.

Being weak from the heat of the sun that had beaten on her for two days, and tired out with hopes and fears, Danae fainted, and knew nothing till she felt cold water on her face. Then she opened her eyes, and saw kind eyes looking at her own, and the brown face of a bearded man, in the light of the blaze that fishermen carry in their boats at night, for the fish come to wonder at it, and the fishermen spear them. There were many dead fish in the boat, into which Danae and the child had been lifted, and a man with a fish spear in his hand was stooping over her.

Then Danae knew that she and her boy were saved, and she lay, unable to speak, till the oarsmen had pulled their boat to a little pier of stone. There the man with the fish spear lifted her up lightly and softly set her on her feet on land, and a boatman handed to him the boy, who was awake, and was crying for food.

'You are safe, lady!' said the man with the spear, 'and I have taken fairer fish than ever swam the sea. I am called Dictys; my brother, Polydectes, is king of this island, and my wife is waiting for me at home, where she will make you welcome, and the boy thrice welcome, for the gods have taken our only son.'

He asked no questions of Danae; it was reckoned ill manners to put questions to strangers and guests, but he lighted two torches at the fire in the boat, and bade his two men walk in front, to show the way, while he supported Danae, and carried the child on his shoulder. They had not far to go, for Dictys, who loved fishing of all things, had his house near the shore. Soon they saw the light shining up

42

from the opening in the roof of the hall; and the wife of Dictys came running out, crying: 'Good sport?' when she heard their voices and footsteps.

'Rare sport,' shouted Dictys cheerily, and he led in Danae, and gave the child into the arms of his wife. Then they were taken to the warm baths, and dressed in fresh raiment. Food was set before them, and presently Danae and Perseus slept on soft beds, with coverlets of scarlet wool.

Dictys and his wife never asked Danae any questions about how and why she came floating on the sea through the night. News was carried quickly enough from the mainland to the islands by fishers in their boats and merchant men, and pedlars. Dictys heard how the king of Argos had launched his daughter and her son on the sea, hoping that both would be drowned. All the people knew in the island, which was called Seriphos, and they hated the cruelty of Acrisius, and many believed that Perseus was the son of Zeus.

If the news from Argos reached Seriphos, we may guess that the news from Seriphos reached Argos, and that Acrisius heard how a woman as beautiful as a goddess, with a boy of the race of the gods, had drifted to the shore of the little isle. Acrisius knew, and fear grew about his heart, fear that was sharper as the years went on, while Perseus was

43

coming to his manhood. Acrisius often thought of ways by which he might have his grandson slain; but none of them seemed safe. By the time when Perseus was fifteen, Acrisius dared not go out of doors, except among the spears of his armed guards, and he was so eaten up by fear that it would have been happier for him if he had never been born.

II. THE VOW OF PERSEUS

It was fortunate for Perseus that Dictys treated him and taught him like his own son, and checked him if he was fierce and quarrelsome, as so strong a boy was apt to be. He was trained in all the exercises of young men, the use of spear and sword, shield and bow; and in running, leaping, hunting, rowing, and the art of sailing a boat. There were no books in Seriphos, nobody could read or write; but Perseus was told the stories of old times, and of old warriors who slew monsters by sea and land. Most of the monsters had been killed, as Perseus was sorry to hear, for he desired to try his own luck with them when he came to be a man. But the most terrible of all, the Gorgons, who were hated by men and gods, lived still, in an island near the Land of the Dead; but the way to that island was unknown. These Gorgons were two sisters, and a third woman; the two were hideous to look on, with hair and wings and claws of bronze, and with teeth like the white tusks of swine. Swinish they were, ugly and loathsome, feeding fearfully on the bodies of unburied men. But the third Gorgon was beautiful save for the living serpents that coiled in her hair. She alone of the three Gorgons was mortal, and could be slain, but who could slay her? So terrible were her eyes that men who had gone up against her were changed into pillars of stone.

This was one of the stories that Perseus heard when he was a boy; and there was a proverb that this or that hard task was 'as difficult to do as to slay the Gorgon.' Perseus, then, ever since he was a little boy, was wondering how he could slay the Gorgon and become as famous as the strong man Heracles, or the good knight Bellerophon, who slew the Chimaera. Perseus was always thinking of such famous men as these, and especially loved the story of Bellerophon.

Perseus was determined to do as great deeds as he. But Perseus was still a boy, and he did not know, and no man could tell him, the way to the island of the Gorgons.

When Perseus was about sixteen years old, the King of Seriphos, Polydectes, saw Danae, fell in love with her, and wanted to take her into his palace, but he did not want Perseus. He was a bad and cruel man, but Perseus was so much beloved by the people that he dared not kill him openly. He therefore made friends with the lad, and watched him carefully to see how he could take advantage of him. The king saw that he was of a rash, daring and haughty spirit, though Dictys had taught him to keep himself well in hand, and that he was eager to win glory. The king fell on this plan: he gave a great feast on his birthday, and invited all the chief men and the richest on the island; Perseus, too, he asked to the banquet. As the custom was, all the guests brought gifts, the best that they had, cattle, women-slaves, golden cups, wedges of gold, great vessels of bronze, and other splendid things, and the king met the guests at the door of his hall, and thanked them graciously.

Last came Perseus: he had no gift to give, for he had nothing of his own. The others began to sneer at him, saying, 'Here is a birthday guest without a birthday gift!' 'How should No Man's son have a present fit for a king.' 'This lad is lazy, tied to his mother; he should long ago have taken service with the captain of a merchant ship.' 'He might at least watch the town's cows on the town's fields,' said another. Thus they insulted Perseus, and the king, watching him with a cruel smile, saw his face grow red, and his blue eyes blaze, as he turned from one

46

to another of the mockers, who pointed their fingers at him and jeered.

At last Perseus spoke: 'Ye farmers and fishers, ye ship-captains and slave dealers of a little isle, I shall bring to your master such a present as none of you dare to seek. Farewell. Ye shall see me once again and no more. I go to slay the Gorgon, and bring such a gift as no king possesses—the Head of the Gorgon.'

They laughed and hooted, but Perseus turned away, his hand on his sword hilt, and left them to their festival, while the king rejoiced in his heart. Perseus dared not see his mother again, but he spoke to Dictys, saying that he knew himself now to be of an age when he must seek his fortune in other lands; and he bade Dictys guard his mother from wrong, as well as he might. Dictys promised that he would find a way of protecting Danae, and he gave Perseus three weighed wedges of gold (which were called 'talents,' and served as money), and lent him a ship, to take him to the mainland of Greece, there to seek his fortune.

In the dawn Perseus secretly sailed away, landed at Malea, and thence walked and wandered everywhere, seeking to learn the way to the island of the Gorgons. He was poorly clad, and he slept at night by the fires of smithies, where beggars and wanderers lay: listening to the stories they told, and asking old people, when he met them, if they knew any one who knew the way to the island of the Gorgons. They all shook their heads. 'Yet I should be near knowing,' said one old man, 'if that isle be close to the Land of the Dead, for I am on its borders. Yet I know nothing. Perchance the dead may know; or the maid that prophesies at Pytho, or the Selloi, the priests with unwashen feet, who sleep on the ground below the sacred oaks of Zeus in the grove of Dodona far away.'

Perseus could learn no more than this, and he wandered on and on. He went to the cave that leads down to the Land of the Dead, where the ghosts answer questions in their thin voices, like the twittering of bats. But the ghosts could not tell him what he desired to know. He went to Pytho, where the maid, in her song, bade him seek the land of men who eat acorns instead of the yellow grain of Demeter, the goddess of harvest. Thence he wandered to Epirus, and to the Selloi who dwell in the oak forest of Zeus, and live on the flour ground from acorns. One of them lay on the ground in the wood, with his head covered up in his mantle, and listened to what the wind says, when it whispers to the forest leaves. The leaves said, 'We bid the young man be of good hope, for the gods are with him.'

This answer did not tell Perseus where the isle of the Gorgons lay, but the words put hope in his heart, weary and footsore as he was. He ate of the bread made of the acorns, and of the flesh of the swine that the Selloi gave him, and he went alone, and, far in the forest, he laid his head down on the broad mossy root of an old oak tree. He did not sleep, but watched the stars through the boughs, and he heard the cries of the night-wandering beasts in the woodland.

'If the gods be with me, I shall yet do well,' he said, and, as he spoke, he saw a white clear light moving through the darkness. That clear white light shone from a golden lamp in the hand of a tall and beautiful woman, clad in armour, and wearing, hung by a belt from her neck, a great shield of polished bronze. With her there came a young man, with winged shoon of gold on his feet, and belted with a strange short curved sword: in his hand was a golden wand, with wings on it, and with golden serpents twisted round it.

Perseus knew that these beautiful folk were the Goddess Athênê, and Hermes, who brings all fortunate things. He fell upon his face before them, but Athênê spoke in a sweet grave voice, saying, 'Arise, Perseus, and speak to us face to face, for we are of your kindred, we also are children of Zeus, the Father of gods and men.'

Then Perseus arose and looked straight into their eyes.

'We have watched you long, Perseus, to learn whether you have the heart of a hero, that can achieve great adventures; or whether you are an idle dreaming boy. We have seen that your heart is steadfast, and that you have sought through hunger, and long travel to know the way wherein you must find death or win glory. That way is not to be found without the help of the gods. First you must seek the Three Grey Women, who dwell beyond the land that lies at the back of the North Wind. They will tell you the road to the three Nymphs of the West, who live in an island of the sea that never knew a sail; for it is beyond the pillars that Heracles set up when he wearied in his journey to the Well of the World's End, and turned again. You must go to these nymphs, where never foot of man has trod, and they will show you the measure of the way to the Isle of the Gorgons. If you see the faces of the Gorgons, you will be turned to stone. Yet you have vowed to bring the head of the youngest of the three, she who was not born a Gorgon but became one of them by reason of her own wickedness. If you slay her, you must not see even her dead head, but wrap it round in this goat-skin which hangs beside my shield; see not the head yourself, and let none see it but your enemies.'

'This is a great adventure,' said Perseus, 'to slay a woman whom I may not look upon, lest I be changed into stone.'

'I give you my polished shield,' said Athênê. 'Let it never grow dim, if you would live and see the sunlight.' She took off her shield from her neck, with the goat-skin cover of the shield, and hung them round the neck of Perseus. He knelt and thanked her for her grace, and, looking up through a clear space between the forest boughs, he said, 'I see the Bear, the stars of the North that are the guide of sailors. I shall walk towards them even now, by your will, for my heart burns to find the Three Grey Women, and learn the way.'

Hermes smiled, and said, 'An old man and white-bearded would you be, ere you measured out that way on foot! Here, take my winged sandals, and bind them about your feet. They know all the paths of the air, and they will bring you to the Three Grey Women. Belt yourself, too, with my sword, for this sword needs no second stroke, but will cleave through that you set it to smite.'

So Perseus bound on the Shoes of Swiftness, and the Sword of Sharpness, the name of it was

Herpê; and when he rose from binding on the shoon, he was alone. The gods had departed. He drew the sword, and cut at an oak tree trunk, and the blade went clean through it, while the tree fell with a crash like thunder. Then Perseus rose through the clear space in the wood, and flew under the stars, towards the constellation of the Bear. North of Greece he flew, above the Thracian mountains, and the Danube (which was then called the Ister) lay beneath him like a long thread of silver. The air grew cold as he crossed lands then unknown to the Greeks, lands where wild men dwelt, clad in the skins of beasts, and using axe-heads and spear-heads made of sharpened stones. He passed to the land at the back of the North Wind, a sunny warm land, where the people sacrifice wild asses to the God Apollo. Beyond this he came to a burning desert of sand, but far away he saw trees that love the water, poplars and willows, and thither he flew.

He came to a lake among the trees, and round and round the lake were flying three huge grey swans, with the heads of women, and their long grey hair flowed down below their bodies, and floated on the wind. They sang to each other as they flew, in a voice like the cry of the swan. They had but one eye among them, and but one tooth, which they passed to each other in turn, for they had arms and hands under their wings. Perseus dropped down in his flight, and watched them. When one was passing the eye to the other, none of them could see him, so he waited for his chance and took it, and seized the eye.

'Where is our eye? Have *you* got it?' said the Grey Woman from whose hand Perseus took it. 'I have it not.'

'I have it not!' cried each of the others, and they all wailed like swans.

'I have it,' said Perseus, and hearing his voice they all flew to the sound of it but he easily kept out of their way. 'The eye will I keep,' said Perseus, 'till you tell me what none knows but you, the way to the Isle of the Gorgons.'

'We know it not,' cried the poor Grey Women. 'None knows it but the Nymphs of the Isle of the West: give us our eye!'

'Then tell me the way to the Nymphs of the Isle of the West,' said Perseus.

'Turn your back, and hold your course past the isle of Albion, with the white cliffs, and so keep with the land on your left hand, and the unsailed sea on your right hand, till you mark the pillars of Heracles on your left, then take your course west by south, and a curse on you! Give us our eye!'

Perseus gave them their eye, and she who took it flew at him, but he laughed, and rose high above them and flew as he was told. Over many and many a league of sea and land he went, till he turned to his right from the Pillars of Heracles (at Gibraltar), and sailed along, west by south, through warm air, over the lonely endless Atlantic waters. At last he saw a great blue mountain, with snow feathering its crests, in a far-off island, and on that island he alighted. It was a country of beautiful flowers, and pine forests high on the hill, but below the pines all was like a garden, and in that garden was a tree bearing apples of gold, and round the tree were dancing three fair maidens, clothed in green, and white, and red.

'These must be the Nymphs of the Isle of the West,' said Perseus, and he floated down into the garden, and drew near them.

As soon as they saw him they left off dancing, and catching each other by the hands they ran to Perseus laughing, and crying, 'Hermes, our play-fellow Hermes has come!' The arms of all of them went round Perseus at once, with much laughing and kissing. 'Why have you brought a great shield, Hermes?' they cried, 'here there is no unfriendly god or man to fight against you.'

Perseus saw that they had mistaken him for

the god whose sword and winged shoon he wore, but he did not dislike the mistake of the merry maidens.

'I am not Hermes,' he said, 'but a mortal man, to whom the god has graciously lent his sword and shoon, and the shield was lent to me by Pallas Athênê. My name is Perseus.'

The girls leaped back from him, blushing and looking shy. The eldest girl answered, 'We are the daughters of Hesperus, the God of the Evening Star. I am Æglê, this is my sister Erytheia, and this is Hesperia. We are the keepers of this island, which is the garden of the gods, and they often visit us; our cousins, Dionysus, the young god of wine and mirth, and Hermes of the Golden Wand come often; and bright Apollo, and his sister Artemis the huntress. But a mortal man we have never seen, and wherefore have the gods sent you hither?'

'The two gods sent me, maidens, to ask you the way to the Isle of the Gorgons, that I may slay Medusa of the snaky hair, whom gods and men detest.'

'Alas!' answered the nymphs, 'how shall you slay her, even if we knew the way to that island, which we know not?'

Perseus sighed: he had gone so far, and endured so much, and had come to the Nymphs of the Isle

55

of the West, and even they could not tell how to reach the Gorgons' island.

'Do not fear,' said the girl, 'for if we know not the way we know one that knows it: Atlas is his name—the Giant of the Mountain. He dwells on the highest peak of the snow-crested hill, and it is he who holds up the heavens, and keeps heaven and earth asunder. He looks over all the world, and over the wide western sea: him we must ask to answer your question. Take off your shield, which is so heavy, and sit down with us among the flowers, and let us think how you may slay the Gorgon.'

Perseus gladly unslung his heavy shield, and sat down among the white and purple wind flowers. Ægle, too, sat down; but young Erytheia held the shield upright, while beautiful Hesperia admired herself, laughing, in the polished surface.

Perseus smiled as he watched them, and a plan came into his mind. In all his wanderings he had been trying hard to think how, if he found the Gorgon, he might cut off her head, without seeing the face which turned men into stone. Now his puzzle was ended. He could hold up the shield above the Gorgon, and see the reflection of her face, as in a mirror, just as now he saw the fair reflected face of Hesperia. He turned to Ægle, who sat silently beside him: 'Maiden,' he said, 'I have found out the secret that has perplexed me long, how I may strike at the Gorgon without seeing her face that turns men to stone. I will hang above her in the air, and see her face reflected in the mirror of the shield, and so know where to strike.' The two other girls had left the shield on the grass, and they clapped their hands when Perseus said this, but Æglê still looked grave.

'It is much that you should have found this cunning plan; but the Gorgons will see you, and two of them are deathless and cannot be slain, even with the sword Herpê. These Gorgons have wings almost as swift as the winged shoon of Hermes, and they have claws of bronze that cannot be broken.'

Hesperia clapped her hands. 'Yet I know a way,' she said, 'so that this friend of ours may approach the Gorgons, yet not be seen by them. You must be told,' she said, turning to Perseus, 'that we three sisters were of the company of the Fairy Queen, Persephone, daughter of Demeter, the Goddess of the Harvest. We were gathering flowers with her, in the plain of Enna, in a spring morning, when there sprang up a new flower, fragrant and beautiful, the white narcissus. No sooner had Persephone plucked that flower than the earth opened beside her, and up came the chariot and horses of Hades, the King of the Dead, who caught Persephone into his chariot, and bore her down with him to the House of Hades. We wept and were in great fear, but Zeus granted to Persephone to return to earth with the first snowdrop, and remain with her mother, Demeter, till the last rose had faded. Now I was the favourite of Persephone, and she carried me with her to see her husband, who is kind to me for her sake, and can refuse me nothing, and he has what will serve your turn. To him I will go, for often I go to see my playmate, when it is winter in your world: it is always summer in our isle. To him I will go, and return again, when I will so work that you may be seen of none, neither by god, or man, or monster. Meanwhile my sisters will take care of you, and to-morrow they will lead you to the mountain top, to speak with the Giant.'

'It is well spoken,' said tall, grave Ægle, and she led Perseus to their house, and gave him food and wine, and at night he slept full of hope, in a chamber in the courtyard.

Next morning, early, Perseus and Ægle and Erytheia floated up to the crest of the mountain, for Hesperia had departed in the night, to visit Queen Persephone. Perseus took a hand of each of the Nymphs, and they had no weary climbing; they all soared up together, so great was the power of the winged shoon of Hermes. They found the good giant Atlas, kneeling on a black rock above the snow, holding up the vault of heaven with either hand. When Ægle had spoken to him, he bade his girls go apart, and said to Perseus, 'Yonder, far away to the west, you see an island with a mountain that rises to a flat top, like a table. There dwell the Gorgons.'

Perseus thanked him eagerly, but Atlas sighed and said, 'Mine is a weary life. Here have I knelt and done my task, since the Giants fought against the gods, and were defeated. Then, for my punishment, I was set here by Zeus to keep sky and earth asunder. But he told me that after hundreds of years I should have rest, and be changed to a stone. Now I see that the day of rest appointed is come, for you shall show me the head of the Gorgon when you have slain her, and my body shall be stone, but my spirit shall be with the ever living gods.'

Perseus pitied Atlas; he bowed to the will of Zeus, and to the prayer of the giant, and gave his promise. Then he floated to Ægle and Erytheia, and they all three floated down again to the garden of the golden apples. Here as they walked on the soft grass, and watched the wind toss the white and red and purple bells of the wind flowers, they heard a low laughter close to them, the laughter of Hesperia, but her they saw not. 'Where are you,

Hesperia, where are you hiding?' cried Æglê, wondering, for the wide lawn was open, without bush or tree where the girl might be lurking.

'Find me if you can,' cried the voice of Hesperia, close beside them, and handfuls of flowers were lightly tossed to them, yet they saw none who threw them. 'This place is surely enchanted,' thought Perseus, and the voice of Hesperia answered:

'Come follow, follow me. I will run before you to the house, and show you my secret.'

Then they all saw the flowers bending, and the grass waving, as if a light-footed girl were running through it, and they followed to the house the path in the trodden grass. At the door, Hesperia met them: 'You could not see me,' she said, 'nor will the Gorgons see Perseus. Look, on that table lies the Helmet of Hades, which mortal men call the Cap of Darkness. While I wore it you could not see me, nay, a deathless god cannot see the wearer of that helmet.' She took up a dark cap of hard leather, that lay on a table in the hall, and raised it to her head, and when she had put it on, she was invisible. She took it off, and placed it on the brows of Perseus. 'We cannot see you, Perseus,' cried all the girls. 'Look at yourself in your shining shield: can you see yourself?'

Perseus turned to the shield, which he had hung

on a golden nail in the wall. He saw only the polished bronze, and the faces of the girls who were looking over his shoulder. He took off the Helmet of Hades and gave a great sigh. 'Kind are the gods,' he said. 'Methinks that I shall indeed keep my vow, and bring to Polydectes the Gorgon's head.'

They were merry that night, and Perseus told them his story, how he was the son of Zeus, and the girls called him 'cousin Perseus.' 'We love you very much, and we could make you immortal, without old age and death,' said Hesperia. 'You might live with us here for ever—it is lonely, sometimes, for three maidens in the garden of the gods. But you must keep your vow, and punish your enemies, and cherish your mother, and do not forget your cousins three, when you have married the lady of your heart's desire, and are King of Argos.'

The tears stood in the eyes of Perseus. 'Cousins dear,' he said, 'never shall I forget you, not even in the House of Hades. You will come thither now and again, Hesperia? But I love no woman.'

'I think you will not long be without a lady and a love, Perseus,' said Erytheia; 'but the night is late, and tomorrow you have much to do.'

So they parted, and next morning they bade Perseus be of good hope. He burnished and polished the shield, and covered it with the goat's skin, he put on the Shoes of Swiftness, and belted himself with the Sword of Sharpness, and placed on his head the Cap of Darkness. Then he soared high in the air, till he saw the Gorgons' Isle, and the table-shaped mountain, a speck in the western sea.

The way was long, but the shoes were swift, and, far aloft, in the heat of the noon-day, Perseus looked down on the top of the table-mountain. There he could dimly see three bulks of strange shapeless shape, with monstrous limbs that never stirred, and he knew that the Gorgons were sleeping their midday sleep. Then he held the shield so that the shapes were reflected in its polished face, and very slowly he floated down, and down, till he was within striking distance. There they lay, two of them uglier than sin, breathing loud in their sleep like drunken men. But the face of her who lay between the others was as quiet as the face of a sleeping child; and as beautiful as the face of the goddess of Love, with long dark eyelashes veiling the eyes, and red lips half open. Nothing stirred but the serpents in the hair of beautiful Medusa; they were never still, but coiled and twisted, and Perseus loathed them as he watched them in the mirror. They coiled and uncoiled, and left bare her ivory neck, and then Perseus drew the sword Herpê, and struck once.

In the mirror he saw the fallen head, and he seized it by the hair, and wrapped it in the goat-skin, and put the goat-skin in his wallet. Then he towered high in the air, and, looking down, he saw the two sister Gorgons turning in their sleep; they woke, and saw their sister dead. They seemed to speak to each other; they looked this way and that, into the bright empty air, for Perseus in the Cap of Darkness they could not see. They rose on their mighty wings, hunting low, and high, and with casts behind their island and in front of it, but Perseus was flying faster than ever he flew before, stooping and rising to hide his scent. He dived into the deep sea, and flew under water as long as he could hold his breath, and then rose and fled swiftly forward. The Gorgons were puzzled by each double he had made, and, at the place where he dived they lost the scent, and from far away Perseus heard their loud yelps, but soon these faded in the distance. He often looked over his shoulder as he flew straight towards the far-off blue hill of the giant Atlas, but the sky was empty behind him, and the Gorgons he never saw again. The mountain turned from blue to clear grey and red and gold, with pencilled rifts and glens, and soon Perseus stood beside the giant Atlas. 'You are welcome and blessed,' said the giant. 'Show me the head that I may be at rest.'

Then Perseus took the bundle from the wallet, and carefully unbound the goat-skin, and held up the head, looking away from it, and the Giant was a great grey stone. Down sailed Perseus, and stood in the garden of the gods, and laid the Cap of Darkness on the grass. The three Nymphs who were sitting there, weaving garlands of flowers, leaped up, and came round him, and kissed him, and crowned him with the flowery chaplets. That night he rested with them, and in the morning they kissed and said farewell.

'Do not forget us,' said Æglê, 'nor be too sorry for our loneliness. To-day Hermes has been with us, and tomorrow he comes again with Dionysus, the god of the vine, and all his merry company. Hermes left a message for you, that you are to fly eastward, and south, to the place where your wings shall guide you, and there, he said, you shall find your happiness. When that is won, you shall turn north and west, to your own country. We say, all three of us, that our love is with you always, and we shall hear of your gladness, for Hermes will tell us; then we too shall be glad. Farewell!'

So the three maidens embraced him with kind faces and smiling eyes, and Perseus, too, smiled as well as he might, but in his eastward way he often looked back, and was sad when he could no longer see the kindly hill above the garden of the gods.

III. PERSEUS AND ANDROMEDA

Perseus flew where the wings bore him, over great mountains, and over a wilderness of sand. Below his feet the wind woke the sand storms, and beneath him he saw nothing but a soft floor of yellow grey, and when that cleared he saw islands of green trees round some well in the waste, and long trains of camels, and brown men riding swift horses, at which he wondered; for the Greeks in his time drove in chariots, and did not ride. The red sun behind him fell, and all the land was purple, but, in a moment, as it seemed, the stars rushed out, and he sped along in the starlight till the sky was grey again, and rosy, and full of fiery colours, green and gold and ruby and amethyst. Then the sun rose, and Perseus looked down on a green land, through which was flowing north a great river, and he guessed that it was the river Ægyptus, which we now call the Nile. Beneath him was a town, with many white houses in groves of palm trees, and with great temples of the gods, built of red stone. The shoes of swiftness stopped above the wide market-place, and there Perseus hung poised, till he saw a multitude of men pour out of the door of a temple.

At their head walked the king, who was like a Greek, and he led a maiden as white as snow wreathed with flowers and circlets of wool, like the oxen in Greece, when men sacrifice them to the gods. Behind the king and the maid came a throng of brown men, first priests and magicians and players on harps, and women shaking metal rattles that made a wild mournful noise, while the multitude lamented.

Slowly, while Perseus watched, they passed down to the shore of the great river, so wide a river as Perseus had never seen. They went to a steep red rock, like a wall, above the river; at its foot was a flat shelf of rock—the water just washed over it. Here they stopped, and the king kissed and embraced the white maiden. They bound her by chains of bronze to rings of bronze in the rock; they sang a strange hymn; and then marched back to the town, throwing their mantles over their heads. There the maiden stood, or rather hung forward supported by the chains. Perseus floated down, and, the nearer he came, the more beautiful seemed the white maid, with her soft dark hair falling to her white feet. Softly he floated down, till his feet were on the ledge of rock. She did not hear

66

him coming, and when he gently touched her she gave a cry, and turned on him her large dark eyes, wild and dry, without a tear. 'Is it a god?' she said, clasping her hands.

'No god, but a mortal man am I. Perseus the slayer of the Gorgon. What do you here? What cruel men have bound you?'

'I am Andromeda, the daughter of Cepheus, king of a strange people. The lot fell on me, of all the maidens in the city, to be offered to the monster fish that walks on feet, who is their god. Once a year they give to him a maiden.'

Perseus thereon drew the sword Herpê, and cut the chains of bronze that bound the girl as if they had been ropes of flax, and she fell at his feet, covering her eyes with her hands. Then Perseus saw the long reeds on the further shore of the river waving and stirring and crashing, and from them came a monstrous fish walking on feet, and slid into the water. His long sharp black head showed above the stream as he swam, and the water behind him showed like the water in the wake of a ship.

'Be still and hide your eyes!' whispered Perseus to the maiden.

He took the goat-skin from his wallet, and held up the Gorgon's head, with the back of it turned towards him, and he waited till the long black head was lifted from the river's edge, and the forefeet of that fish were on the wet ledge of rock. Then he held the head before the eyes of the monster, and from the head downward it slowly stiffened. The head and forefeet and shoulders were of stone before the tail had ceased to lash the water. Then the tail stiffened into a long jagged sharp stone, and Perseus, wrapping up the head in the goat-skin, placed it in his wallet. He turned his back to Andromeda, while he did this lest by mischance her eyes should open and see the head of the Gorgon. But her eyes were closed, and Perseus found that she had fainted, from fear of the monster, and from the great heat of the sun. Perseus put the palms of his hands together like a cup, and stooping to the stream he brought water, and threw it over the face and neck of Andromeda, wondering at her beauty. Her eyes opened at last, and she tried to rise to her feet, but she dropped on her knees, and clung with her fingers to the rock. Seeing her so faint and weak Perseus raised her in his arms, with her beautiful head pillowed on his shoulder, where she fell asleep like a tired child. Then he rose in the air and floated over the sheer wall of red stone above the river, and flew slowly towards the town.

There were no sentinels at the gate; the long street was empty, for all the people were in their houses, praying and weeping. But a little girl stole out of a house near the gate. She was too young to understand why her father and mother and elder brothers were so sad, and would not take any notice of her. She thought she would go out and play in the street, and when she looked up from her play, she saw Perseus bearing the king's daughter in his arms. The child stared, and then ran into her house, crying aloud, for she could hardly speak, and pulled so hard at her mother's gown that her mother rose and followed her to the house door. The mother gave a joyful cry, her husband and her children ran forth, and they, too, shouted aloud for pleasure. Their cries reached the ears of people in other houses, and presently all the folk, as glad as they had been sorrowful, were following Perseus to the palace of the king. Perseus walked through the empty court, and stood at the door of the hall, where the servants came to him, both men and women, and with tears of joy the women bore Andromeda to the chamber of her mother, Queen Cassiopeia.

Who can tell how happy were the king and queen, and how gladly they welcomed Perseus! They made a feast for him, and they sent oxen and sheep to all the people, and wine, that all might rejoice and make merry. Andromeda, too, came, pale but smiling, into the hall, and sat down beside her mother's high seat, listening while Perseus told the whole story of his adventures. Now Perseus could scarcely keep his eyes from Andromeda's face while he spoke, and she stole glances at him. When their eyes met, the colour came into her face again, which glowed like ivory that a Carian woman has lightly tinged with rose colour, making an ornament for some rich king. Perseus remembered the message of Hermes, which Æglê had given him, that if he flew to the east and south he would find his happiness. He knew that he had found it, if this maiden would be his wife, and he ended his tale by repeating the message of Hermes.

'The gods speak only truth,' he said, 'and to have made you all happy is the greatest happiness to Perseus of Argos.' Yet he hoped in his heart to see a yet happier day, when the rites of marriage should be done between Andromeda and him, and the young men and maidens should sing the wedding song before their door.

Andromeda was of one mind with him, and, as Perseus just needs go home, her parents believed that she could not live without him who had saved her from such a cruel death. So with heavy hearts they made the marriage feast, and with many tears Andromeda and her father and mother said farewell.

Perseus and his bride sailed down the great river Ægyptus in the king's own boat; and at every town they were received with feasts, and songs, and dances. They saw all the wonderful things of Egypt, palaces and pyramids and temples and tombs of kings, and at last they found a ship of the Cretans in the mouth of the Nile. This they hired, for they carried with them great riches, gold, and myrrh, and ivory, gifts of the princes of Egypt.

IV. HOW PERSEUS AVENGED DANAE

With a steady south wind behind them they sailed to Seriphos, and landed, and brought their wealth ashore and went to the house of Dictys. They found him lonely and sorrowful, for his wife had died, and his brother, King Polydectes, had taken Danae, and set her to grind corn in his house, among his slave women. When Perseus heard that word, he asked, 'Where is King Polydectes?'

'It is his birthday, and he holds his feast among the princes,' said Dictys.

'Then bring me,' said Perseus, 'the worst of old clothes that any servant of your house can borrow from a begged man, if there be a beggar man in the town.' Such a man there was—he came limping through the door of the courtyard, and up to the threshold of the house, where he sat whining, and asking for alms. They gave him food and wine, and Perseus cried, 'New clothes for old, father, I will give you, and new shoes for old.' The beggar could not believe his ears, but he was taken to the baths, and washed, and new clothes were given to him, while Perseus clad himself in the beggar's rags, and Dictys took charge of the winged shoon of Hermes and the sword Herpê, and the burnished shield of Athênê. Then Perseus cast dust and wood ashes on his hair, till it looked foul and grey, and placed the goat-skin covering and the Gorgon's head in his wallet, and with the beggar's staff in his hand he limped to the palace of Polydectes. On the threshold he sat down, like a beggar, and Polydectes saw him and cried to his servants, 'Bring in that man; is it not the day of my feast? Surely all are welcome.' Perseus was led in, looking humbly at the ground, and was brought before the king.

'What news, thou beggar man?' said the king.

'Such news as was to be looked for,' whined Perseus. 'Behold, I am he who brought no present to the king's feast, seven long years agone, and now I come back, tired and hungry, to ask his grace.'

'By the splendour of Zeus,' cried Polydectes, 'it is none but the beggar brat who bragged that he would fetch me such a treasure as lies in no king's chamber! The beggar brat is a beggar man; how time and travel have tamed him! Ho, one of you, run and fetch his mother who is grinding at the mill, that she may welcome her son.'

A servant ran from the hall, and the chiefs of Seriphos mocked at Perseus. 'This is he who called us farmers and dealers in slaves. Verily he would not fetch the price of an old cow in the slave market.' Then they threw at him crusts of bread, and bones of swine, but he stood silent.

Then Danae was led in, clad in vile raiment, but looking like a queen, and the king cried, 'Go forward, woman: look at that beggar man; dost thou know thy son?' She walked on, her head high, and Perseus whispered, 'Mother, stand thou beside me, and speak no word!'

'My mother knows me not, or despises me,' said Perseus, 'yet, poor as I am, I do not come empty-handed. In my wallet is a gift, brought from very far away, for my lord the king.'

He swung his wallet round in front of him; he took off the covering of goat-skin, and he held the Gorgon's head on high, by the hair, facing the king and the chiefs. In one moment they were all grey stones, all along the hall and the chairs whereon they sat crashed under the weight of them, and they rolled on the hard clay floor. Perseus wrapped the head in the goat-skin, and shut it in the wallet carefully, and cried, 'Mother, look round, and see thy son and thine own revenge.'

Then Danae knew her son, by the sound of his voice, if not by her eyesight, and she wept for joy. So they two went to the house of Dictys, and Perseus was cleansed, and clad in rich raiment, and Danae, too, was apparelled like a free woman, and embraced Andromeda with great joy.

Perseus made the good Dictys king of Seriphos; and he placed the winged shoes in the temple of Hermes, with the sword Herpê, and the Gorgon's head, in its goat-skin cover; but the polished shield he laid on the altar in the temple of Athênê. Then he bade all who served in the temples come forth, both young and old, and he locked the doors, and he and Dictys watched all night, with the armed Cretans, the crew of his ship, that none might enter. Next day Perseus alone went into the temple of Athênê. It was as it had been, but the Gorgon's head and the polished shield were gone, and the winged shoon and the sword Herpê had vanished from the temple of Hermes.

With Danae and Andromeda Perseus sailed to Greece, where he learned that the sons of King Proetus had driven King Acrisius out of Argos, and that he had fled to Phthia in the north, where the ancestor of the great Achilles was king. Thither

Perseus went, to see his grandfather, and he found the young men holding games and sports in front of the palace. Perseus thought that his grandfather might love him better if he showed his strength in the games, which were open to strangers, so he entered and won the race, and the prize for leaping, and then came the throwing disc of bronze. Perseus threw a great cast, far beyond the rest, but the disc swerved, and fell among the crowd. Then Perseus was afraid, and ran like the wind to the place where the disc fell. There lay an old man, smitten sorely by the disc, and men said that he had killed King Acrisius.

Thus the word of the prophetess and the will of Fate were fulfilled. Perseus went weeping to the King of Phthia, and told him all the truth, and the king, who knew, as all Greece knew, how Acrisius had tried to drown his daughter and her child, believed the tale, and said that Perseus was guiltless. He and Danae and Andromeda dwelt for a year in Phthia, with the king, and then Perseus with an array of Pelasgians and Myrmidons, marched south to Argos, and took the city, and drove out his cousins, the sons of Proetus. There in Argos Perseus, with his mother and beautiful Andromeda, dwelt long and happily, and he left the kingdom to his son when he died.

HERACLES

The Greek hero Heracles is often better known today by his Latin name, Hercules. Whichever name he goes by, however, he remains one of the most well-known heroes of ancient Greek myth. The number of stories in which he features are greater than most, for even to the ancients he was one of their most renowned figures. In this version, Emilie Kip Baker strings together an impressive number of his adventures from infancy to his death, including his famous twelve labours. Heracles's life was a troubled one, however, and many of the trials he faced were due to the anger of his stepmother Hera. For Heracles was the son of Zeus by a mortal woman, not Hera. While Hera's fury was with her husband and his numerous affairs, punishing the king of the gods was a near impossible feat, so instead Heracles became her convenient target.

I

Heracles was the son of Zeus and Alcmene—a
lovely princess, the granddaughter of Perseus and
Andromeda. Hera hated her as she did all her
mortal rivals, and sought to bring misery and suf-
fering on the unoffending maiden. When she
learned that Heracles, the son of Alcmene, was
born, she sent two immense serpents with poisonous fangs to attack the child while he slept. The
baby happened to waken just as the creatures were
twining themselves about him; and grasping their
necks in each of his tiny hands, he strangled them,
thus showing from his birth the wonderful strength
that was later to make him a famous hero. The
education of Heracles was intrusted to Chiron, the
most renowned of the centaurs, who had himself
been instructed by Apollo and Artemis in hunting,
medicine, music, and the art of prophecy. The idea
of a creature half man and half horse was not
repulsive to the ancients, who were too fond of a
horse to consider man's union with him degrading.
When Heracles left the kindly tutelage of Chiron,

he set out on his own adventures, and before he had traveled far he met two beautiful women, each of whom offered to guide him on his journey. Kakia (Vice) told him that if he followed her, he would gain love, riches, and ease; and Arete (Virtue) promised him honor, bought at the price of hardship, poverty, and endless toil. For a while the youthful hero deliberated over the two very different rewards offered him, and at last he gave his choice to Arete, who henceforth led him through many perils, and into labors such as no man had ever yet performed.

Like most heroes, Heracles was a great wanderer; and on one of his journeys he came to the city of Thebes, where Creon, the king, entertained him and showed him so much favor that when Heracles asked for the hand of Creon's daughter Megara in marriage, the king gladly gave his consent. The hero then rested from his wanderings, and spent many happy years in the society of his wife and children; but Hera had not forgotten her old hatred of Alcmene's offspring, and she determined to end this happiness. So she afflicted Heracles with a sudden madness; and in his delirium he killed his wife, and threw his children into the fire. When at last he recovered his senses, he suffered terribly over the thought of the crimes that he had unwittingly committed, and would have gone off to the mountains to spend his days in sorrow and remorse, had not Hera demanded that he should expiate his deeds of bloodshed. Accordingly she sent Hermes to lead him from his solitude among the hills and to take him to his cousin Eurystheus, king of Argos, whom he was compelled to serve for a whole year. During this time he performed the twelve great labors that have made his name famous as the doer of mighty deeds.

The first task that Eurystheus gave the hero was to procure the skin of a monstrous lion that inhabited the Nemean forest. This creature's frequent attacks had brought terror to all the countryside, for it was not content with carrying off cattle and sheep, but had killed the children at play, and mangled shepherds who were watching with their flocks. When the people heard that Heracles was setting out to fight the lion, they tried to persuade him to give up the adventure; but he, who had strangled two huge serpents in his infancy, was not afraid of a lion, however fierce and strong it might be. So he boldly entered the forest, and having tracked the great brute to its den, he attacked it fearlessly and killed it with his bare hands. Then, throwing the body of the lion over his shoulder, he started back to the palace of Eurystheus; but when the king saw Heracles approaching, he begged him to leave his burden outside the city gates. So the hero skinned the lion, and took the shaggy pelt to be henceforth his favorite covering.

Heracles's second labor was to kill the Hydra, a nine-headed monster that infested the marshes of Lerna. With the blows of his great oak club the hero was able to strike off eight of the heads, but the central one was immortal and could not be destroyed. Further to complicate the difficulty, Heracles found that as soon as he struck off one head, two others sprang up in its place. To prevent this discouraging miracle from continuing, the hero bade his friend Iolaus, who had accompanied him, take a lighted brand and sear the wounds as soon as they were made. Through this wise precaution the Hydra was finally killed, and its one immortal head was buried under a huge rock. While this difficult struggle was going on, Hera, always eager to thwart the hero, sent a large crab to pinch Heracles's feet as he wrestled with the Hydra. He succeeded in crushing it with his club; but Hera did not leave its body on the trampled and blood-stained ground. In recognition of its services to her, she placed it in the sky as the constellation of Cancer (the Crab). Before Heracles left the dead Hydra he dipped some arrows in its venomous blood, knowing that any wound received from their poisoned tips would surely be fatal. These arrows were later of great service to Heracles, and only once did he regret their deadly quality.

The next task that Eurystheus set was the capture of the golden-horned and brazen-hoofed stag of Cerynea, which ran so swiftly that it did not seem to touch the ground. Heracles pursued the stag for many miles, but was unable to overtake it until he drove it into the cold regions of the north, where its fleetness was hindered by the great drifts and the ice-covered ground. Finally the stag ran into a deep snow bank, and so Heracles captured it and took it home in triumph.

The fourth labor to which Heracles lent his great strength was the killing of a wild boar that haunted Mount Erymanthus in Arcadia. While on this expedition, the hero was attacked by the centaurs, and when he shot at them with his poisoned arrows, one of the deadly missiles flew far and struck his loved tutor Chiron, who was galloping toward the combatants, hoping to settle the quarrel peaceably. When Heracles saw Chiron fall, he rushed to his side and tried to stanch the fatal wound; but the dying centaur knew that his end had come, and sorrowfully bade the hero farewell.

To reward Chiron for his long service, the gods transferred him to the heavens as the constellation Sagittarius.

Heracles was next sent to kill the flock of fierce birds whose cruel beaks and sharp talons made havoc in the country around Lake Stymphalus. The foul mist that rose from the stagnant water over which the birds hovered was so deadly to breathe that Heracles could hardly approach the lake; but with the help of his poisoned arrows he was able to wound the birds at a distance. After hours spent in this pestilent atmosphere he killed the entire flock and returned to the court of Eurystheus to report his success.

The most unpleasant of all Heracles's labors was the cleaning of the stables where Augeas, king of Elis, kept his herd of a thousand oxen. These stables had not been cleaned for thirty years; and when Heracles caught one glimpse of the filth within them, he felt that this was too degrading a task for him to undertake. But the work had to be done; and since he could not put his hand to anything so foul, he looked about for some other means to accomplish the labor. Not far from the stables flowed two rivers, the Peneus and Alpheus, and these Heracles turned out of their courses and made them rush through the filthy building until every part of the stables of Augeas was washed perfectly clean. Then he restored the rivers to their former beds, and returned home to report this task fulfilled.

The next labor that was assigned to the hero was the capture of a mad bull given by Neptune to King Minos. In the early days of his power, Minos had boasted that he could obtain anything that he wished from the gods; and had accordingly begged of Neptune a bull for the sacrifices. The kindly sea-god sent a splendid offering, but when Minos saw the bull's size and beauty, he resolved to keep it. So he substituted another animal for the sacrifices. This angered Neptune so much that he made the bull go mad; and it rushed here and there over the island, causing great terror among the people. The creature was finally caught and overcome by Heracles, who rode it through the waves to Greece. The offspring of this bull was the famous Mino-taur which the hero Theseus pursued through its labyrinth, and slew.

The eighth labor of Heracles was to bring from Thrace the horses of Diomedes. These splendid creatures the king fed on human flesh; and in order to get a sufficient supply of fresh meat, he decreed that all strangers who came into his kingdom should be imprisoned, fattened up, and then served as food to the horses. To punish Diomedes for his years of cruelty, Heracles fed him to his own steeds, and then led them back to Eurystheus, who was proud to be the possessor of such a prize.

At the court of Eurystheus was the king's beautiful daughter, Admete, who loved purple and fine linen, and decked herself with all the jewels that her father's wealth could command. One day Admete heard a traveler telling wonderful tales of the girdle that was worn by Hippolyte, queen of the Amazons; and at once the spoiled princess demanded of her father that he send Heracles to procure for her the coveted girdle. So the hero set out again, accompanied by his friend Iolaus; and after a hard and perilous journey came to the country of the Amazons. These were a fierce, warlike nation of women who kept in their tribe only the girls who were born among them and disposed of the boys by killing them, or by giving them to the neighboring peoples. The girls were trained in severe military discipline, and became a race of very redoubtable warriors whom no king cared to treat with contempt. When Heracles came before the queen Hippolyte, she received him kindly, listened to the explanation of his visit, and even promised to give him the girdle that the selfish Admete coveted. Before the hero and his friend set out on their journey homeward, the queen entertained them royally with feasting and games that lasted several days. Meantime Hera saw an opportunity for indulging her hatred of Heracles; and taking the form of an Amazon, she mingled freely with the women. By pretending to have received a heaven-sent message, she persuaded them that the stranger had used the girdle as a mere pretext for his visit, and that his real intention was to carry off the queen. The Amazons believed this artfully-contrived report, and rushed in a body to protect Hippolyte. They attacked Heracles fiercely, but he beat them off and finally escaped with his friend, but not before he had killed several of the Amazons, including the queen who had befriended him. With the dearly-bought girdle he returned homeward, and on the way he heard the proclamation of Laomedon that whoever would save his daughter Hesione from the sea-monster should receive a large reward. Heracles killed the beast and freed the maiden, but was obliged to leave Troy without the promised gold, because of Laomedon's perfidy and greed.

When the ancients looked each evening at the glowing west, they pictured it as a far-distant country, more wonderful than any ever seen by mortal eyes. Here in this land of heart's desire lay the

Garden of the Hesperides, where a dragon guarded the golden apples that grew on a wonderful tree which had sprung up miraculously to grace the wedding of Zeus and Hera. In this far-off sunset land were also the Isles of the Blest, where mortals who had led virtuous lives were transported without ever tasting of death. Here the blessed of the gods enjoyed an eternity of bliss; and wandered happily over the Isles, which had a sun and moon and stars of their own, and never felt the touch of wintry winds. In this mysterious region of the west was the island of Erythea, called "the red" because it glowed in the light of the setting sun. To this spot Heracles was sent to take possession of the oxen of Geryon—a monster with three bodies. On his journey to the island, Heracles's way was blocked by a huge mountain; and with one blow of his strong oak club he cleft the opposing rock, and allowed the waters of the sea to flow through. This is now the strait of Gibraltar, and the cliffs on either side are called the Pillars of Heracles.

When the hero reached the island of Erythea, he found the oxen guarded by the giant Eurytion and his three-headed dog; but even this did not daunt the slayer of the Hydra. He boldly attacked the giant; and after a fierce battle, in which his oak club stood him in good stead, killed both Eurytion and the monstrous dog. Then he went in search of the oxen, and, after herding them closely, drove them toward his own country. On the journey homeward he passed Mount Aventine, where the giant Cacus lived in a rocky cave. One night, as Heracles was asleep near the mountain, the giant stole part of the cattle; and, to deceive the hero, he dragged them backwards by their tails into his cave. Heracles might have been tricked by this stratagem if the stolen oxen had not lowed loudly as the rest of the herd passed the cave, and so betrayed their hiding place. Heracles rushed into the giant's dark, ill-smelling dwelling, slew him, and recovered all the stolen cattle.

II

One of the most difficult of Heracles's labors was to procure the golden apples that the Hesperides, daughters of Hesperus, god of the west, guarded very jealously. At the foot of the tree coiled a fierce dragon whose nostrils poured out fire, and whose deadly breath would have slain any venturesome robber, even if he had escaped the dragon's claws. As Heracles did not know in what part of the great glowing west the Garden of the Hesperides lay, he wandered many miles before he met with any one who could direct him where to go. The first help he received was from the nymphs of the Eridanus River, who were sporting on the river bank and called to Heracles to come and join in their games. Much as he would have liked to rest, the hero dared not tarry; but he begged the friendly nymphs to tell him the way to the Garden of the Hesperides. They could not help him, but they advised him to go to old Proteus, "the Ancient of the Deep," who could tell him whatever he wished to know better than any one else. So Heracles went down to the seashore, and found the hoary god asleep in his cool green cave. Knowing the old man's wiles, the hero grasped him firmly and held him fast through all the bewildering changes by which he sought to frighten away the stranger. At last, finding himself securely caught, the Wizard assumed his own form, and asked Heracles what it was that he wished to know. The hero stated his errand, and Proteus told him, "in words that ne'er deceive," that he must find the giant Atlas who alone knew where the Garden of the Hesperides lay.

Heracles then started again on his search, and in the course of his journey came to the Caucasus Mountains, where he found Prometheus, the stealer of the sacred fire, bound with adamantine chains to the rock, while a vulture daily feasted on his liver. Heracles killed the foul bird, broke the chains, and set Prometheus free; and in return for his deliverance the grateful Titan directed his rescuer where to find the giant Atlas. Following Prometheus's advice, Heracles traveled straightway to Africa; and on the way he passed through the land of the Pygmies, a tiny race of warriors who waged continual warfare with neighboring tribes, and especially with their deadly enemies, the cranes. Heracles was not aware that he had reached the country of the Pygmies; but one day, when he had fallen asleep from weariness, he was wakened by sharp prickings over his body; and looking around he saw a host of diminutive men, attacking him with their tiny weapons. The hero laughed at these brave efforts, caught up a few of the doughty little warriors, and, wrapping them in his lion skin, carried them back with him to the court of Eurystheus.

As he journeyed through Africa in search of Atlas, Heracles came to the country of Anteus—a mighty giant and wrestler, and the son of Terra, the Earth. All strangers who came into the land were obliged to wrestle with him, and if they were defeated, they were immediately killed. As no one had ever overcome Anteus, he had brought an untimely death on many a brave hero; so Heracles was eager to defeat him and avenge the unknown dead. As soon as they had grappled for the first struggle, the slayer of the Hydra knew that he had met more than his equal in strength. For a long time they wrestled, Anteus growing stronger after each fall, and Heracles growing fainter from every additional blow of the giant's hand. Again and again the undaunted hero threw his adversary to the ground, but Anteus rose with redoubled vigor and continued the unequal contest. Then, all at once, Heracles remembered the tale he had once heard told of a giant who drew strength from his mother Earth; and believing that this was the case with Anteus, he made a mighty effort and lifted the giant from the ground. Anteus struggled to get his feet again on the earth; but Heracles kept him in the air, and held him there until he felt the powerful body beginning to weaken. Little by little the miraculous strength oozed away, and soon Anteus grew so weak that Heracles easily crushed the limp form with his hands.

The hero then traveled on in search of Atlas, whom he finally found standing on the coast of Africa, with the great weight of the heavens resting on his broad shoulders. As Heracles looked up at the enormous figure, which reached so far into the clouds that nothing could be seen above his waist, he noticed that the forests had grown up so thick and tall all around that only a glimpse of the giant's huge legs could be seen through the heavy foliage. As the hero stood watching this figure that for centuries had stood here in obedience to the divine command of Zeus, he saw dark clouds beginning to gather about the giant's head, and soon a storm broke over the sea and land. Amid the beating of the rain and the crash of the thunder, Heracles thought he heard the voice of Atlas speaking to him; but it might have been only a peal of thunder. When the storm was over and the mists rolled away from the earth, Heracles saw the head of Atlas through rifts in the scurrying clouds. The snow-white hair gave the giant's face a benign look as it fell thick and white over the stooping shoulders that bore so terrible a weight. In a voice that he strove hard to make gentle, Atlas asked the hero what he was seeking, and Heracles told him that he had come to get some of the golden apples from the Garden of the Hesperides. Atlas laughed at these words, and his great shoulders shook so with merriment that a few of the stars fell out of their places. Then he told Heracles that such a feat was impossible even to so great a hero; but that if some one would take the heavens from his shoulders for a few hours, he himself would get the apples.

Heracles was delighted with this offer of assistance, and agreed to take the giant's burden while the latter went on his friendly errand. Very carefully Atlas transferred the heavens to the shoulders of Heracles, and then sped westward to the Garden of the Hesperides. The hero was a bit troubled when he saw Atlas shake his huge shoulders and stretch himself in delight at his freedom, for it would be strange, indeed, if the giant were ready to resume his burden after having tasted the joy of liberty. With some anxiety Heracles watched him step into the sea that came only to his knees though he had waded out a mile from the shore. As Atlas went deeper and deeper into the waves, at first his huge bulk loomed like a cliff against the horizon; but soon it dwindled into a mere speck, and was presently lost to view. How long he stood holding the heavens Heracles never knew; but he found himself growing very weary of his burden, and anxious over Atlas's long absence. Suddenly he saw a dark spot on the horizon, and he knew that it was the giant returning.

It had not been a difficult task for Atlas to reach the Garden, or to pluck the golden apples from the carefully-guarded tree; and Heracles, delighted with the giant's success, thanked him for his trouble and asked him politely to take the sky again on his shoulders, for the journey back to the court of Eurystheus was a long one. Now Atlas had no desire to stand for another dozen centuries with his old burden; and seeing a good opportunity of getting rid of it forever, he told Heracles that he would carry the apples to Eurystheus himself; and meanwhile the hero could keep the heavens supported until Atlas returned. Pretending that he was quite satisfied with this arrangement, Heracles bade the giant good-by; then hastily asked him to wait a moment while he made a pad for his shoulders to ease the weight of the unaccustomed burden. The unsuspicious giant good-naturedly agreed to this, and took the heavens from Heracles; but instead of making a cushion, the hero picked up the golden apples, which Atlas had dropped on resuming his burden, and started back to his own country, leaving the giant to stand on the seashore forever, or until the pitying gods should release him.

The twelfth and last labor of Heracles was to bring from Hades the three-headed dog, Cerberus. With the help of Hermes and Minerva, he descended into the dread realm of Hades, and begged that grim monarch to let him take Cerberus into the upper world. Hades was not willing at first to lose the guardian of his gates even for a short time; but at length he consented to let

Heracles do as he desired on condition that Cerberus should not be bound or any weapons used upon him. So the fierce three-headed creature was carried, snarling and struggling, in the hero's strong arms; and when the pair approached the throne of Eurystheus, the horror-struck monarch implored Heracles to take the monster back as quickly as possible, for the sight of its dripping jaws, from which oozed the deadly nightshade, so terrified Eurystheus that he sought refuge in a huge jar, and would not come out until his courtiers assured him that Cerberus was safely out of the country.

When the twelve labors were ended, Heracles's term of service at the court of Eurystheus was over, and he was free to wander where he willed. He spent many years roaming through various lands and assisting other heroes who, like himself, were in search of adventures. He took part in the battle between the Centaurs and Lapithæ; joined in the Argonautic expedition; organized the first siege of Troy, and braved the terrors of Hades to bring Alcestis back to her repentant husband. The expedition against Troy was one of revenge, for the false Laomedon had never paid the gold that he had promised for the release of his daughter Hesione from the sea monster; and Heracles now set out to punish the treacherous king. So he sailed for Troy with eighteen ships, and the city fell into his hands with but little resistance. Laomedon was killed, his son Priam placed on the throne of Troy, and Hesione given in marriage to Telamon, one of the Greeks who accompanied Heracles.

The hero's splendid career received a check, however, for in a quarrel he killed his friend Iphitus, and the gods, angry at this unnecessary bloodshed, compelled him to go once more into bondage. So for three years Heracles served Omphale, queen of Lydia; and during this time he lived very effeminately, wearing sometimes the dress of a woman and spinning wool with the handmaidens of Omphale, while the queen wore his lion's skin and wielded his renowned club. When his years of servitude were over, he set out again on his wanderings; and during one of his journeys he met the beautiful Deïaneira, daughter of Œneus of Calydon and sister of Meleager, famous in the Calydonian hunt. Heracles immediately sought the maiden's hand in marriage; but she had another suitor, the river god Achelous, who had already obtained her father's consent. Deïaneira, however, much preferred her new lover, and begged him to free her from the betrothal with Achelous. So Heracles challenged the river-god to a wrestling match, the conditions of the contest being that he who won should have the maiden in marriage. Achelous readily agreed to this way of settling their rival pretensions, for he had no doubt as to the result of the wrestling.

The opponents were well matched as to strength, but the river-god had one great advantage, for he could assume any form he pleased, and thus bewilder any one who tried to grapple with him. Among his many changes, he took the form of a serpent; but when Heracles grasped it by the neck and was about to strangle it, Achelous became a bull and rushed at the hero with lowered horns. Skillfully eluding this unexpected attack, Heracles seized the bull by one horn and held on so firmly that when the creature tried to wrench himself free the horn broke. This decided the victory in favor of Heracles, and Achelous departed sullenly to his bed in the river. The broken horn was appropriated by Tyche, the goddess of plenty, who filled it with her treasures, and adopted it thenceforth as her symbol, calling it Cornucopia.

There was nothing now to hinder the marriage of Heracles with Deïaneira, and the wedding took place with much mirth and feasting. After several days of festivity Heracles departed with his wife; and in the course of their journey homeward, they came to the river Evenus, which had grown so swollen and turbid from the heavy rains that it was impossible to ford it. As the travelers stood helpless on the bank, the centaur Nessus came galloping up to them, and offered to carry Deïaneira across the river in safety. Grateful for this timely assistance, Heracles placed his wife on the back of the centaur, who swam with her through the swift-flowing stream. When they reached the opposite bank, Deïaneira expected the centaur to stop, that she might dismount; but Nessus set off at a brisk trot, hoping to kidnap his fair rider before her husband could overtake them. Heracles heard the cries of his terrified bride, and as soon as he swam the river he sent a swift arrow after the treacherous Nessus. The poisoned tip sank deep into the centaur's side, and he knew at once that he had received his death-wound. With a pretense at repentance, he asked Deïaneira to forgive his rash deed; and then, as if granting her a favor, he told her to take his robe which was stained with blood, and keep it carefully, for it had wonderful properties. He assured her that if the time ever came that Heracles's love grew cold, she had only to persuade him to put on this magic robe, and his devotion to her would become more ardent than ever before. Deïaneira took the robe, but said nothing to her husband of the centaur's gift, hoping that she would never have to make use of it.

For many years Heracles and his wife lived happily together; for, although the hero went on other adventures, he was always eager to return to Deïaneira, and she had no need to be reminded of the centaur's gift. On one of his expeditions, however, he brought back with him a fair maiden named Iole, of whom his wife soon grew to be extremely jealous. Not long after the arrival of Iole, Heracles wished to offer sacrifices to the gods in honor of his safe return; so he sent to Deïaneira for a suitable robe. His wife, trembling for the success of her venture, bade the messenger Lichas carry to Heracles the magic robe of Nessus, which she had carefully guarded all these years. The hero, not knowing the history of the fatal garment, threw it over his shoulders, and as soon as it touched his flesh, the poisoned blood began its deadly work. The body of Heracles burned suddenly as if on fire, and agonizing pains convulsed his frame. He tried to unloose the fatal robe, but it clung to his skin, and he tore off part of his flesh in trying to set himself free. In his rage and pain he turned upon Lichas, the unhappy bearer of the poisoned robe, and seizing him in his still powerful arms flung him into the sea from the top of Mount Œta, where they had assembled for the sacrifices. Then the hero tore up huge oak trees by their roots and built a lofty funeral pyre on which he stretched his pain-wracked limbs. Calmly he bade his servants apply the torch, but no one was willing to do this, even to ease his sufferings; so Heracles turned to his friend Philoctetes, and after giving him the poisoned arrows, begged him in pity to light the funeral pyre. The youth placed beside Heracles the hero's famous oak club, and covered his body with the lion's skin. Then he applied a torch to the wood, and the flames rose with a roar and cracking to the skies. But only the mortal part of the hero perished, for Zeus would not allow the divinity that he had bestowed upon Heracles to suffer extinction. Purged of his mortality, the hero took his place in high Olympus, and even revengeful Hera was so reconciled to his presence, that she gave him her daughter Hebe in marriage.

ADMETUS AND ALCESTIS

The myth of Admetus and Alcestis features one of the more blissfully romantic unions in Greek myth. Admetus was king of Pherae, in Thessaly, and was married to a woman named Alcestis. Admetus was a fair and kind king while Alcestis was a brave and noble queen. Unsurprisingly, they were both beloved by their people. It was their love for one another, however, that makes their tale so memorable. When Alcestis sees her husband on death's door, she is willing to sacrifice herself on behalf of Ademetus and their people. Josephine Preston Peabody recounts their story in her retelling, while reminding us that not all acts of heroism involve wielding swords or slaying fearsome monsters. Alcestis becomes a heroine in a somewhat different way.

Apollo did not live always free of care, though he was the most glorious of the gods. One day, in anger with the Cyclopes who work at the forges of Hephaestus, he sent his arrows after them, to the wrath of all the gods, but especially of Zeus. (For the Cyclopes always make his thunderbolts, and make them well.) Even the divine archer could not go unpunished, and as a penalty he was sent to serve some mortal for a year. Some say one year and some say nine, but in those days time passed quickly; and as for the gods, they took no heed of it.

Now there was a certain king in Thessaly, Admetus by name, and there came to him one day a stranger, who asked leave to serve about the palace. None knew his name, but he was very comely, and moreover, when they questioned him he said that he had come from a position of high trust. So without further delay they made him chief shepherd of the royal flocks.

Every day thereafter, he drove his sheep to the banks of the river Amphrysus, and there he sat to watch them browse. The country-folk that passed drew near to wonder at him, without daring to ask questions. He seemed to have a knowledge of leechcraft, and knew how to cure the ills of any wayfarer with any weed that grew near by; and he would pipe for hours in the sun. A simple-spoken man he was, yet he seemed to know much more than he would say, and he smiled with a kindly mirth when the people wished him sunny weather.

Indeed, as days went by, it seemed as if summer had come to stay, and, like the shepherd, found the place friendly. Nowhere else were the flocks so white and fair to see, like clouds loitering along a bright sky; and sometimes, when he chose, their keeper sang to them. Then the grasshoppers drew near and the swans sailed close to the river banks, and the countrymen gathered about to hear wonderful tales of the slaying of the monster Python, and of a king with ass's ears, and of a lovely maiden, Daphne, who grew into a laurel-tree. In time the rumor of these things drew the king himself to listen; and Admetus, who had been to see the world in the ship Argo, knew at once that this was no earthly shepherd, but a god. From that day, like a true king, he treated his guest with reverence and friendliness, asking no questions; and the god was well pleased.

Now it came to pass that Admetus fell in love with a beautiful maiden, Alcestis, and, because of the strange condition that her father Pelias had laid upon all suitors, he was heavy-hearted. Only that man who should come to woo her in a chariot drawn by a wild boar and a lion might ever marry Alcestis; and this task was enough to puzzle even a king.

As for the shepherd, when he heard of it he rose, one fine morning, and left the sheep and went his way,—no one knew whither. If the sun had gone out, the people could not have been more dismayed. The king himself went, late in the day, to walk by the river Amphrysus, and wonder if his gracious keeper of the flocks had deserted him in a time of need. But at that very moment, whom should he see returning from the woods but the shepherd, glorious as sunset, and leading side by side a lion and a boar, as gentle as two sheep! The very next morning, with joy and gratitude, Admetus set out in his chariot for the kingdom of Pelias, and there he wooed and won Alcestis, the most loving wife that was ever heard of.

It was well for Admetus that he came home with such a comrade, for the year was at an end, and he was to lose his shepherd. The strange man came to take leave of the king and queen whom he had befriended.

"Blessed be your flocks, Admetus," he said, smiling. "They shall prosper even though I leave them. And, because you can discern the gods that come to you in the guise of wayfarers, happiness shall never go far from your home, but ever return to be your guest. No man may live on earth forever, but this one gift have I obtained for you. When your last hour draws near, if any one shall be willing to meet it in your stead, he shall die, and you shall live on, more than the mortal length of days. Such kings deserve long life."

So ended the happy year when Apollo tended sheep.

For many years the remembrance of Apollo's service kept Thessaly full of sunlight. Where a god could work, the people took heart to work also. Flocks and herds throve, travellers were befriended, and men were happy under the rule of a happy king and queen.

But one day Admetus fell ill, and he grew weaker and weaker until he lay at death's door. Then, when no remedy was found to help him and the hope of the people was failing, they remembered the promise of the Fates to spare the king if some one else would die in his stead. This seemed a simple matter for one whose wishes are law, and whose life is needed by all his fellow-men. But, strange to say, the substitute did not come forward at once.

Among the king's most faithful friends, many were afraid to die. Men said that they would gladly give their lives in battle, but that they could not die in bed at home like helpless old women. The wealthy had too much to live for; and the poor, who possessed nothing but life, could not bear to give up that. Even the aged parents of Admetus shrunk from the thought of losing the few years that remained to them, and thought it impious that any one should name such a sacrifice.

All this time, the three Fates were waiting to cut the thread of life, and they could not wait longer.

Then, seeing that even the old and wretched clung to their gift of life, who should offer herself but the young and lovely queen, Alcestis? Sorrowful but resolute, she determined to be the victim, and made ready to die for the sake of her husband.

She took leave of her children and commended them to the care of Admetus. All his pleading could not change the decree of the Fates. Alcestis prepared for death as for some consecration. She bathed and anointed her body, and, as a mortal illness seized her, she lay down to die, robed in fair raiment, and bade her kindred farewell. The household was filled with mourning, but it was too late. She waned before the eyes of the king, like daylight that must be gone.

At this grievous moment Heracles, mightiest of all men, who was journeying on his way to new adventures, begged admittance to the palace, and inquired the cause of such grief in that hospitable place. He was told of the misfortune that had befallen Admetus, and, struck with pity, he resolved to try what his strength might do for this man who had been a friend of gods.

Already Death had come out of Hades for Alcestis, and as Heracles stood at the door of her chamber he saw that awful form leading away the lovely spirit of the queen, for the breath had just departed from her body. Then the might that he had from his divine father Zeus stood by the hero. He seized Death in his giant arms and wrestled for victory.

Now Death is a visitor that comes and goes. He may not tarry in the upper world; its air is not for him; and at length, feeling his power give way, he loosed his grasp of the queen, and, weak with the struggle, made escape to his native darkness of Hades.

In the chamber where the royal kindred were weeping, the body of Alcestis lay, fair to see, and once more the breath stirred in her heart, like a waking bird. Back to its home came her lovely spirit, and for long years after she lived happily with her husband, King Admetus.

THE CALYDONIAN HUNT
AND ATALANTA

Heroines in Greek myth come in many different forms, and they include prodigious huntresses and warriors like the princess Atalanta. Like many a Greek heroine, Atalanta had a rough start in life, abandoned by her father, King of Arcadia, because of her sex, and adopted by a bear. Despite all this, however, she finds her way in the wilderness and grows up to become the greatest huntress among men and women, second only to the goddess Artemis herself. Here Jean Lang recounts Atalanta's most famous myths, providing readers with a glimpse into not only the heroine's strength, but her cunning mind. While both the ancient Greeks and author Jean Lang might liken her courage to that of a man, as modern readers we can see that Atalanta was simply an impressive woman with no need to be compared with anyone other than herself.

Œneus and Althæa were king and queen of Calydon, and to them was born a son who was his mother's joy and yet her bitterest sorrow. Meleager was his name, and ere his birth his mother dreamed a dream that the child that she bore was a burning firebrand. But when the baby came he was a royal child indeed, a little fearless king from the first moment that his eyes, like unseeing violets, gazed steadily up at his mother. To the chamber where he lay by his mother's side came the three Fates, spinning, ceaselessly spinning.

"He shall be strong," said one, as she span her thread. "He shall be fortunate and brave," said the second. But the third laid a billet of wood on the flames, and while her withered fingers held the fatal threads, she looked with old, old, sad eyes at the newborn child.

"To thee, O New-Born," she said, "and to this wood that burns, do we give the same span of days to live."

From her bed sprang Althæa, and, heedless of the flames, she seized the burning wood, trod on it with her fair white feet, and poured on it water that swiftly quenched its red glow. "Thou shalt live forever, O Beloved," she said, "for never again shall fire char the brand that I have plucked from the burning."

And the baby laughed.

> "Those grey women with bound hair
> Who fright the gods frighted not him; he laughed
> Seeing them, and pushed out hands to feel and haul
> Distaff and thread."

The years sped on, and from fearless and beautiful babyhood, Meleager grew into gallant boyhood, and then into magnificent youth. When Jason and his heroes sailed away into a distant land to win the Golden Fleece, Meleager was one of the noble band. From all men living he won great praise for his brave deeds, and when the tribes of the north and west made war upon Ætolia, he fought against their army and scattered it as a wind in autumn drives the fallen leaves before it.

But his victory brought evil upon him. When his father Œneus, at the end of a fruitful year, offered sacrifices to the gods, he omitted to honour the goddess Artemis by sacrificing to her, and to punish his neglect, she had sent this destroying army. When Meleager was victor, her wrath against his father grew yet more hot, and she sent a wild boar, large as the bulls of Epirus, and fierce and savage to kill and to devour, that it might ravage and lay waste the land of Calydon. The fields of corn were trampled under foot, the vineyards laid waste, and the olive groves wrecked as by a winter hurricane. Flocks and herds were slaughtered by it, or driven hither and thither in wild panic, working havoc as they fled. Many went out to slay it, but went only to find a hideous death. Then did Meleager resolve that he would rid the land of this monster, and called on all his friends, the heroes of Greece, to come to his aid. Theseus and his friend Pirithous came; Jason; Peleus, afterwards father of Achilles; Telamon, the father of Ajax; Nestor, then but a youth; Castor and Pollux, and Toxeus and Plexippus, the brothers of Althæa, the fair queen-mother. But there came none more fearless nor more ready to fight the monster boar of Calydon than Atalanta, the daughter of the king of Arcadia. When Atalanta was born, her father heard of her birth with anger. He desired no daughter, but only sturdy sons who might fight for him, and in the furious rage of bitter disappointment he had the baby princess left on the Parthenian Hill that she might perish there. A she-bear heard the baby's piteous cries, and carried it off to its lair, where she suckled it along with her young, and there the little Atalanta tumbled about and played with her furry companions and grew strong and vigorous as any other wild young creature of the forest.

Some hunters came one day to raid the den and kill the foster-mother, and found, amazed, a fearless, white-skinned thing with rosy cheeks and brave eyes, who fought for her life and bit them as did her fierce foster-brothers, and then cried human tears of rage and sorrow when she saw the bear who had been her mother lying bloody and dead. Under the care of the hunters Atalanta grew into a maiden, with all the beauty of a maid and all the strength and the courage of a man. She ran as swiftly as Zephyrus runs when he rushes up from the west and drives the white clouds before him like a flock of timid fawns that a hound is pursuing. The shafts that her strong arm sped from her bow smote straight to the heart of the beast that she chased, and almost as swift as her arrow was she there to drive her spear into her quarry. When at length her father the king learned that the beautiful huntress, of whom all men spoke as of one only a little lower than Artemis, was none other than his daughter, he was not slow to own her as his child. So proud was he of her beauty and grace, and of her marvellous swiftness of foot and skill in the chase, that he would fain have married her to one of the great ones of Greece, but Atalanta had consulted an oracle. "Marry not," said the oracle. "To thee marriage must bring woe."

So, with untouched heart, and with the daring and the courage of a young lad, Atalanta came along with the heroes to the Calydonian Hunt. She was so radiantly lovely, so young, so strong, so courageous, that straightway Meleager loved her, and all the heroes gazed at her with eyes that adored her beauty. And Artemis, looking down at her, also loved the maiden whom from childhood she had held in her protection—a gallant, fearless virgin dear to her heart.

The grey mist rose from the marshes as the hunt began, and the hunters of the boar had gone but a little way when they came upon traces of the hated boar. Disembowelled beasts marked its track. Here, in a flowery meadow, had it wallowed. There, in rich wheat land, had it routed, and the marks of its bestial tusks were on the gashed grey trunks of the trees that had once lived in the peace of a fruitful olive grove.

In a marsh they found their enemy, and all the reeds quivered as it heaved its vast bulk and hove aside the weed in which it had wallowed, and rooted with its tusks amongst the wounded water-lilies before it leapt with a snort to meet and to slay the men who had come against it. A filthy thing it was, as its pink snout rose above the green ooze of the marshes, and it looked up lustily, defying the purity of the blue skies of heaven, to bring to those who came against it a cruel, shameful death.

Upon it, first of all, Jason cast his spear. But the sharp point only touched it, and unwounded, the boar rushed on, its gross, bristly head down, to disembowel, if it could, the gallant Nestor. In the branches of a tree Nestor found safety, and Telamon rushed on to destroy the filthy thing that would have made carrion of the sons of the gods. A straggling cypress root caught his fleeting foot and laid him prone, a helpless prey for the rooting brute. His hounds fell before it, but ere it could reach him, Atalanta, full of vengeful rage—the pure angered against the filthy and cruel—let draw her bow, with a prayer to Artemis to guide her shaft aright. Into the boar's smoking flank sped the arrow.

"The sudden string
Rang, and sprang inward, and the waterish air
Hissed, and the moist plumes of the songless reeds
Moved as a wave which the wind moves no more.
But the boar heaved half out of ooze and slime,

His tense flank trembling round the barbed wound,
Hateful; and fiery with invasive eyes
And bristling with intolerable hair
Plunged, and the hounds clung, and green flowers
    and white
Reddened and broke all round them where they
    came.
And charging with sheer tusk he drove, and smote
Hyleus; and sharp death caught his sudden soul,
And violent sleep shed night upon his eyes."

—SWINBURNE.

More than ever terrible was the monster now that it was wounded. One after the other the hunters fell before its mad rage, and were sent to the shades by a bloody and merciless death.

Before its furious charge even the heart of a hero might have been stricken. Yet Meleager, like a mighty oak of the forest that will not sway even a little before the rush of a storm, stood full in its way and met its onslaught.

"Aimed on the left side his well-handled spear
Grasped where the ash was knottiest hewn, and
    smote,
And with no missile wound, the monstrous boar
Right in the hairiest hollow of his hide

Under the last rib, sheer through bulk and bone,

Deep in; and deeply smitten, and to death,

The heavy horror with his hanging shafts,

Leapt, and fell furiously, and from raging lips

Foamed out the latest wrath of all his life."

Great was the shout that rose from those who still lived when that grim hunt thus came to an end. And when, with his keen blade, Meleager struck off the head, even as the quivering throat drew its last agonised breath, louder still shouted the men of Greece. But not for himself did Meleager despoil the body of his foe. He laid the ugly thing at the feet of Atalanta.

"This is thy spoil, not mine," he said. "The wounding shaft was sped by thee. To thee belongs the praise."

And Atalanta blushed rosily, and laughed low and gladly, not only because Artemis had heard her prayer and helped her slay the beast, but for happiness that Meleager was so noble in his giving.

At that the brows of the heroes grew dark, and angrily one cried:

"Lo, now,

Shall not the Arcadian shoot out lips at us,

Saying all we were despoiled by this one girl."

Like a spark that kindles the dry grass, their kindling anger spread, and they rushed against Atalanta, seized the trophy she had been given, and smote her as though she were but a shameless wanton and not the noble daughter of a king.

And because the heart of Meleager was given very wholly to the fair huntress, and because those whom he deemed his friends had not only dishonoured her, but had done him a very grievous wrong, a great rage seized him. Right and left he smote, and they who had been most bitter in their jealousy of Atalanta, the two brothers of his own mother, were laid low in death.

Tidings of the slaying of the boar had been brought to Althæa by swift messengers, and she was on her way to the temples bearing gifts to the gods for the victory of her son, when she beheld the slow-footed procession of those who bore the bodies of the dead. And when she saw the still faces of her two dear brothers, quickly was her joy turned into mourning. Terrible was her grief and anger when she learned by whose hand they were slain, and her mother's love and pride dried up in her heart like the clear water of a fountain before the scorching of a devouring fire. No sacrifices to the gods would she offer, but her dead brothers should have the greatest sacrifice that mother could make to atone for the guilt of her son. Back to the palace she went, and from its safe hiding-place drew out the brand that she had rescued from the flames when Meleager the hero was but a babe that made his mother's heart sing for joy. She commanded a fire to be prepared, and four times, as its flames blazed aloft, she tried to lay the brand upon the pile. Yet four times she drew back, and then at last she threw into the reddest of the ashes the charred brand that for a little she held so close to her breast that it seemed as though she fondled her child.

A wreath of leaves as sign of victory was being placed on Atalanta's beautiful head by the adoring hands of Meleager when his mother gave him his doom. Through his body there rushed a pang of mortal agony. His blood turned to fire, and the hand of Death that smote him was as a hand of molten lead. In torture his gallant spirit passed away, uncomplaining, loving through his pain the maid for whose dear sake he had brought woe upon himself. As the last white ashes in the fire crumbled and fell away into nothingness, the soul of Meleager departed. Swiftly through the dark valley his mother's shade followed him, for she fell upon a sword and so perished. And Artemis, looking down on the grief-stricken sisters of Meleager and on the bitter sorrow of his father, had compassion on them and turned them into birds.

So ended the Calydonian Hunt, and Atalanta returned to Arcadia, heavy at heart for the evil she had wrought unwittingly. And still the Three Fates span on, and the winds caught up the cold wood ashes and blew them across the ravaged land that Meleager had saved and that quickly grew fertile again.

Atalanta, daughter of the king of Arcadia, returned sad at heart to her own land. Only as comrades, as those against whose skill in the chase she was wont to pit her own skill, has she looked upon men. But Meleager, the hero who loved her and her fair honour more than life itself, and whose love had made him haste in all his gallant strength and youthful beauty to the land of the Shades, was one to touch as she had never before had she been touched. Her father, proud of her triumph in Calydon, again besought her to marry one of her many noble suitors.

"If indeed they love me as thou sayest," said Atalanta to her father, "then must they be ready to face for my sake even the loss of dear life itself. I shall be the prize of him who outruns me in a foot-race. But he who tries and fails, must pay to Death his penalty."

Thereafter, for many days, a strange sight was to be seen in Arcadia. For one after another the suitors came to race with the maiden whose face had bewitched them, though truly the race was no more fair to him who ran than would be a race with Death. No mortal man was a fleet as Atalanta, who had first raced with the wild things of the mountains and the forests, and who had dared at last to race with the winds and leave even them behind. To her it was all a glorious game. Her conquest was always sure, and if the youths who entered in the contest cared to risk their lives, why should they blame her? So each day they started, throbbing hope and fierce determination to win her in the heart of him who ran—fading hope and despairing anger as he saw her skimming ahead of him like a gay-hued butterfly that a tired child pursues in vain. And each day, as the race ended, another man paid the price of his defeat.

Daily, amongst those who looked on, stood her cousin Milanion. He would fain have hated Atalanta for her ruthlessness and her joyousness as he saw his friends die for her sake, yet daily her beauty, her purity, and her gallant unconsciousness took a firmer hold upon his heart. To himself he vowed that he would win Atalanta, but not without help from the gods was this possible. Therefore he sought Aphrodite herself and asked her aid.

Milanion was a beautiful youth, and to Aphrodite, who loved beauty, he pled his cause as he told her how Atalanta had become to him more than life, so that he had ceased to pity the youths, his friends, who had died for love of her. The goddess smiled upon him with gentle sympathy.

In the garden of her temple grew a tree with branches and twigs of gold, and leaves as yellow as the little leaves of the silver birch when the autumn sun kisses them as it sets. On this tree grew golden apples, and Aphrodite plucked three of them and gave them to the youth who had not feared to ask her to aid him to win the maid he loved. How he was to use the apples she then told him, and, well content, Milanion returned home.

Next day he spoke to Atalanta.

"So far has victory been thine, Fairest on earth," he said, "but so far have thy little winged white feet had only the heavy-footed laggards to outrun. Wilt have me run a race with thee? for assuredly I shall win thee for my own."

And Milanion looked into the eyes of Atalanta

with a smile as gay and fearless as that with which a hero is wont to look in the eyes of his fellow.

Look for look did the virgin huntress give him.

Then her cheeks grew red, as though the rosy-fingered dawn had touched them, and the dawning of love came into her heart.

Even Meleager was not quite so goodly a youth as this. Not even Meleager had been so wholly fearless.

"Thou art tempted by the deathless gods," she said, but her long lashes drooped on her cheek as she spoke. "I pity you, Milanion, for when thou dost race with me, the goal is assuredly the meadows of asphodel near where sit Hades and Persephone on their gloomy thrones."

But Milanion said, "I am ready, Atalanta. Wilt thou race with me now?" And steadily he looked in her eyes until again they fell as though at last they had found a conqueror.

Like two swallows that skim across a sunny sea, filled with the joyousness of the coming of spring, Atalanta and Milanion started. Scarcely did their feet seem to touch the solid earth, and all those who stood by vowed that now, at length, was a race indeed, a race worthy for the gods to behold.

But as they ran, almost abreast, so that none could tell which was the gainer, Milanion obeyed the bidding of Aphrodite and let fall one of the golden apples. Never before had Atalanta dreamed of such a thing—an apple of glistening gold! She stopped, poised on one foot as a flying bird poises for a moment on the wing, and picked up the treasure. But Milanion had sped several paces ahead ere she was again abreast of him, and even as she gained on him, he dropped the second apple. Again Atalanta was tempted. Again she stopped, and again Milanion shot ahead of her. Her breath came short and fast, as once more she gained the ground that she had lost. But, yet a third time, Milanion threw in her way one of the golden illusions of the gods. And, yet again, Atalanta stopped to pick up the apple of gold.

Then a mighty shout from those who watched rent the air, and Atalanta, half fearful, half ashamed, yet wholly happy, found herself running, vanquished, into the arms of him who was indeed her conqueror. For not only had Milanion won the race, but he had won the heart of the virgin huntress, a heart once as cold and remote as the winter snow on the peak of Mount Olympus.

THE FLEECE OF GOLD

This next story is the story of Jason, and it opens with the golden ram. The ram was either a creation of or an incarnation of the goddess Nephele, and from its golden fleece jutted two large wings. On its back, the son of Nephele, known as Phrixus, escaped his evil stepmother and flew to Colchis, home of King Aeetes. After Aeetes offers Phrixus haven, the young man sacrifices the creature and gifts its golden fleece to the king. It is this same fleece that Jason is given the impossible task of retrieving by his villainous uncle. As you will read, Jason sets sale to Colchis on a ship named the *Argo* with a band of strapping heroes, including Heracles himself. The *Argo*'s crew of heroes take on the name the Argonauts from the Greek for sailor and thus, we meet the famous Jason and the Argonauts.

THE SEARCH FOR THE FLEECE

Some years after the Golden Ram died in Colchis, far across the sea, a certain king reigned in Iolcos in Greece, and his name was Pelias. He was not the rightful king, for he had turned his stepbrother, King Æson, from the throne, and taken it for himself. Now, Æson had a son, a boy called Jason, and he sent him far away from Pelias, up into the mountains. In these hills there was a great cave, and in that cave lived Chiron the Wise, who, the story says, was half a horse. He had the head and breast of a man, but a horse's body and legs. He was famed for knowing more about everything than anyone else in all Greece. He knew about the stars, and the plants of earth, which were good for medicine and which were poisonous. He was the best archer with the bow, and the best player of the harp; he could sing songs and tell stories of old times, for he was the last of a people, half horse and half man, who had dwelt in ancient days on the hills. Therefore the kings in Greece sent their sons to him to be taught shooting, singing, and telling the truth, and that was all the teaching they had then, except that they learned to hunt, fish, and fight, and throw spears, and toss the hammer and the stone. There Jason lived with Chiron and the boys in the cave, and many of the boys became famous.

There was Orpheus who played the harp so sweetly that wild beasts followed his minstrelsy, and even the trees danced after him, and settled where he stopped playing. There was Mopsus who could understand what the birds say to each other; and there was Butes, the handsomest of men; and Tiphys, the best steersman of a ship; and Castor, with his brother Polydeuces, the boxer. Heracles, too, the strongest man in the whole world, was there; and Lynceus, whom they called Keen-eye, because he could see so far, and could see even the dead men in their graves under the earth. There was Ephemus, so swift and light-footed that he could run upon the gray sea and never wet his feet; and there were Calais and Zetes, the two sons of the North Wind, with golden wings upon their feet. There also was Peleus, who later married Thetis of the silver feet, goddess of the sea foam, and was the father of Achilles. Many others were there whose names it would take too long to tell. They all grew up together in the hills good friends, healthy, and brave, and strong. And they all went out to their own homes at last; but Jason had no home to go to, for his uncle, Pelias, had taken it, and his father was a wanderer.

So at last he wearied of being alone, and he said good-bye to his teacher, and went down through the hills toward Iolcos, his father's old home, where his wicked uncle Pelias was reigning. As he went, he came to a great, flooded river, running red from bank to bank, rolling the round boulders along. And there on the bank was an old woman sitting.

'Cannot you cross, mother?' said Jason; and she said she could not, but must wait until the flood fell, for there was no bridge.

'I'll carry you across,' said Jason, 'if you will let me carry you.'

So she thanked him, and said it was a kind deed, for she was longing to reach the cottage where her little grandson lay sick.

Then he knelt down, and she climbed upon his back, and he used his spear for a staff, and stepped into the river. It was deeper than he thought, and stronger, but at last he staggered out on the farther bank, far below where he went in. And then he set the old woman down.

'Bless you, my lad, for a strong man and a

brave!' she said, 'and my blessing go with you to the world's end.'

Then he looked and she was gone he did not know where, for she was the greatest of the goddesses, Hera, the wife of Zeus, who had taken the shape of an old woman, to try Jason, whether he was kind and strong, or rude and churlish. From this day her grace went with him, and she helped him in all dangers.

Then Jason went down limping to the city, for he had lost one shoe in the flood. And when he reached the town he went straight up to the palace, and through the court, and into the open door, and up the hall, where the king was sitting at his table among his men. There Jason stood, leaning on his spear.

When the king saw him he turned white with terror. For he had been told by the prophetess of Pytho that a man with only one shoe would come some day and take away his kingdom. And here was the half-shod man of whom the prophecy had spoken.

But Pelias still remembered to be courteous, and he bade his men lead the stranger to the baths, and there the attendants bathed him, pouring hot water over him. And they anointed his head with oil, and clothed him in new raiment, and brought him back to the hall, and set him down at a table beside the king, and gave him meat and drink.

When he had eaten and was refreshed, the king said: 'Now it is time to ask the stranger who he is, and who his parents are, and whence he comes to Iolcos?'

And Jason answered, 'I am Jason, son of the rightful king, Æson, and I am come to take back my kingdom.'

The king grew pale again, but he was cunning, and he leaped up and embraced the lad, and made much of him, and caused a gold circlet to be twisted in his hair. Then he said he was old, and weary of judging the people. 'And weary work it is,' he said, 'and no joy therewith shall any king have. For there is a curse on the country, that shall not be taken away till the Fleece of Gold is brought home, from the land of the world's end. The ghost of Phrixus stands by my bedside every night, wailing and will not be comforted, till the Fleece is brought home again.'

When Jason heard that he cried, 'I shall take the curse away, for by the splendour of Lady Hera's brow, I shall bring the Fleece of Gold from the land of the world's end before I sit on the throne of my father.'

Now this was the very thing that the king

wished, for he thought that if once Jason went after the Fleece, certainly he would never come back living to Iolcos. So he said that it could never be done, for the land was far away across the sea, so far that the birds could not come and go in one year, so great a sea was that and perilous. Also, there was a dragon that guarded the Fleece of Gold, and no man could face it and live.

But the idea of fighting a dragon was itself a temptation to Jason, and he made a great vow by the water of Styx, an oath the very gods feared to break, that certainly he would bring home that Fleece to Iolcos. And he sent out messengers all over Greece, to all his old friends, who were with him in the Centaur's cave, and bade them come and help him, for that there was a dragon to kill, and that there would be fighting. And they all came, driving in their chariots down dales and across hills: Heracles, the strong man, with the bow that none other could bend; and Orpheus with his harp, and Castor and Polydeuces, and Zetes and Calais of the golden wings, and Tiphys, the steersman, and young Hylas, still a boy, and as fair as a girl, who always went with Heracles the strong.

These came, and many more, and they set shipbuilders to work, and oaks were felled for beams, and ashes for oars, and spears were made, and arrows feathered, and swords sharpened. But in the prow of the ship they placed a bough of an oak tree from the forest of Zeus in Dodona where the trees can speak, and that bough spoke, and prophesied things to come. They called the ship 'Argo,' and they launched her, and put bread, and meat, and wine on board, and hung their shields outside the bulwarks. Then they said good-bye to their friends, went aboard, sat down at the oars, set sail, and so away eastward to Colchis, in the land of the world's end.

All day they rowed, and at night they beached the ship, as was then the custom, for they did not sail at night, and they went on shore, and took supper, and slept, and next day to the sea again. And old Chiron, the man-horse, saw the swift ship from his mountain heights, and ran down to the beach; there he stood with the waves of the gray sea breaking over his feet, waving with his mighty hands, and wishing his boys a safe return. And his wife stood beside him, holding in her arms the little son of one of the ship's company, Achilles, the son of Peleus of the Spear, and of Thetis the goddess of the Sea Foam.

So they rowed ever eastward, and ere long they came to a strange isle where dwelt men with six hands apiece, unruly giants. And these giants lay in wait for them on cliffs above the river's mouth where the ship was moored, and before the dawn they rolled down great rocks on the crew. But Heracles drew his huge bow, the bow for which he slew Eurytus, king of Oechalia, and wherever a giant showed hand or shoulder above the cliff, he pinned him through with an arrow, till all were slain. After that they still held eastward, passing many islands, and towns of men, till they reached Mysia, and the Asian shore. Here they landed, with bad luck. For while they were cutting reeds and grass to strew their beds on the sands, young Hylas, beautiful Hylas, went off with a pitcher in his hand to draw water. He came to a beautiful spring, a deep, clear, green pool, and there the water-fairies lived, whom men called Nereids. There were Eunis, and Nycheia with her April eyes, and when they saw the beautiful Hylas, they longed to have him always with them, to live in the crystal caves beneath the water, for they had never seen anyone so beautiful. As he stooped with his pitcher and dipped it into the stream, they caught him softly in their arms, and drew him down below, and no man ever saw him any more, but he dwelt with the water-fairies.

But Heracles the strong, who loved him like a younger brother, wandered all over the country crying '*Hylas! Hylas!*' and the boy's voice answered so faintly from below the stream that Heracles never heard him. So he roamed alone in the forests, and the rest of the crew thought he was lost.

Then the sons of the North Wind were angry, and bade them set sail without him, and sail they did, leaving the strong man behind. Long afterward, when the Fleece was won, Heracles met the sons of the North Wind, and slew them with his arrows. And he buried them, and set a great stone on each grave, and one of these is ever stirred, and shakes when the North Wind blows. There they lie, and their golden wings are at rest.

Still they sped on, with a west wind blowing, and they came to a country whose king was strong, and thought himself the best boxer then living, so he came down to the ship and challenged anyone of that crew; and Polydeuces, the boxer, took up the challenge. All the rest, and the people of the country, made a ring, and Polydeuces and huge King Amycus stepped into the midst, and put up their hands. First they moved round each other cautiously, watching for a chance, and then, as the sun shone forth in the Giant's face, Polydeuces leaped in and struck him between the eyes with his left hand, and, strong as he was, the Giant staggered and fell. Then his friends picked him up, and sponged his face with water, and all the crew of 'Argo' shouted with joy. He was soon on his feet again, and rushed at Polydeuces, hitting out so hard that he would have killed him if the blow had gone home. But Polydeuces just moved his head a little on one side, and the blow went by, and, as the Giant slipped, Polydeuces planted one in his mouth and another beneath his ear, and was away before the Giant could recover.

There they stood, breathing heavily, and glaring at each other, till the Giant made another rush, but Polydeuces avoided him, and struck him several blows quickly in the eyes, and now the Giant was almost blind. Then Polydeuces at once ended the combat by a right-hand blow on the temple. The Giant fell, and lay as if he were dead. When he came to himself again, he had no heart to go on, for his knees shook, and he could hardly see. So Polydeuces made him swear never to challenge strangers again as long as he lived, and then the crew of 'Argo' crowned Polydeuces with a wreath of poplar leaves, and they took supper, and Orpheus sang to them, and they slept, and next day they came to the country of the unhappiest of kings.

His name was Phineus, and he was a prophet; but, when he came to meet Jason and his company, he seemed more like the ghost of a beggar than a crowned king. For he was blind, and very old, and he wandered like a dream, leaning on a staff, and feeling the wall with his hand. His limbs all trembled, he was but a thing of skin and bone, and foul and filthy to see. At last he reached the doorway of the house where Jason was, and sat down, with his purple cloak fallen round him, and he held up his skinny hands, and welcomed Jason, for, being a prophet, he knew that now he should be delivered from his wretchedness.

He lived, or rather lingered, in all this misery because he had offended the gods, and had told men what things were to happen in the future beyond what the gods desired that men should know. So they blinded him, and they sent against him hideous monsters with wings and crooked claws, called Harpies, which fell upon him at his meat, and carried it away before he could put it to his mouth. Sometimes they flew off with all the meat; sometimes they left a little, that he might not quite starve, and die, and be at peace, but might live in misery. Yet what they left was made so foul, and of such evil savour, that even a starving man could scarcely take it within his lips. Thus this king was the most miserable of all men living.

He welcomed the heroes, and, above all, Zetes and Calais, the sons of the North Wind, for they, he knew, would help him. And they all went into his wretched, naked hall, and sat down at the tables, and the servants brought meat and drink and placed it before them, the latest and last supper of the Harpies. Then down on the meat swooped the Harpies, like lightning or wind, with clanging brazen wings, and iron claws, and the smell of a battlefield where men lie dead; down they swooped, and flew shrieking away with the food. But the two sons of the North Wind drew their short swords, and rose in the air on their golden wings, and followed where the Harpies fled, over many a sea and many a land, till they came to a distant isle, and there they slew the Harpies with their swords. And that isle was called 'Turn Again,' for there the sons of the North Wind turned, and it was late in the night when they came back to the hall of Phineus, and to their companions.

Here Phineus was telling Jason and his company how they might win their way to Colchis and the world's end, and the wood of the Fleece of Gold. 'First,' he said, 'you shall come in your ship to the Rocks Wandering, for these rocks wander like living things in the sea, and no ship has ever sailed between them. They open, like a great mouth, to let ships pass, and when she is between their lips they clash again, and crush her in their iron jaws. By this way even winged things may never pass; nay, not even the doves that bear ambrosia to Father Zeus, the lord of Olympus, but the rocks ever catch one even of these. So, when you come near them, you must let loose a dove from the ship, and let her go before you to try the way. And if she flies safely between the rocks from one sea to the other sea, then row with all your might when the rocks open again. But if the rocks close on the bird, then return, and do not try the adventure. But, if you win safely through, then hold right on to the mouth of the River Phasis, and there you shall see the towers of Æêtes, the king, and the grove of the Fleece of Gold. And then do as well as you may.'

So they thanked him, and the next morning they set sail, till they came to a place where the Rocks Wandering wallowed in the water, and all was foam; but when the Rocks leaped apart the stream ran swift, and the waves roared beneath the rocks, and the wet cliffs bellowed. Then Euphemus took the dove in his hands, and set her free, and she flew straight at the pass where the rocks met, and sped right through, and the rocks gnashed like gnashing teeth, but they caught only a feather from her tail.

Then slowly the rocks opened again, like a wild beast's mouth that opens, and Tiphys, the helmsman, shouted, 'Row on, hard all!' and he held the ship straight for the pass. Then the oars bent like bows in the hands of men, and the good ship leaped at the stroke. Three strokes they pulled, and at each the ship leaped, and now they were within the black jaws of the rocks, the water boiling round them, and so dark it was that overhead they could see the stars, but the oarsmen could not see the daylight behind them, and the steersman could not see the daylight in front. Then the great tide rushed in between the rocks like a rushing river, and lifted the ship as if it were lifted by a hand, and through the strait she passed like a bird, and the rocks clashed, and only broke the carved wood of the ship's stern. And the ship reeled into the seething sea beyond, and all the men of Jason bowed their heads over their oars, half dead with the fierce rowing.

Then they set all sail, and the ship sped merrily on, past the shores of the inner sea, past bays and towns, and river mouths, and round green hills, the tombs of men slain long ago. And, behold, on the top of one mound stood a tall man, clad in rusty armour, and with a broken sword in his hand, and on his head a helmet with a blood-red crest. Thrice he waved his hand, and thrice he shouted aloud, and was no more seen, for this was the ghost of Sthenelus, Actæon's son, whom an arrow had slain there long since, and he had come forth from his tomb to see men of his own blood, and to greet Jason and his company. So they anchored there, and slew sheep in sacrifice, and poured blood and wine on the grave of Sthenelus. There Orpheus left a harp, placing it in the bough of a tree, that the wind might sing in the chords, and make music to Sthenelus below the earth.

Then they sailed on, and at evening they saw above their heads the snowy crests of Mount Caucasus, flushed in the sunset; and high in the air they saw, as it were, a black speck that grew greater and greater, and fluttered black wings, and then fell sheer down like a stone. Then they heard a dreadful cry from a valley of the mountain, for there Prometheus was fastened to the rock, and the eagles fed upon him, because he stole fire from the gods, and gave it to men. All the heroes shuddered when they heard his cry; but not long after Heracles came that way, and he slew the eagle with his bow, and set Prometheus free.

But at nightfall they came into the wide mouth of the River Phasis, that flows through the land of the world's end, and they saw the lights burning in the palace of Æêtes the king. So now they were come to the last stage of their journey, and there they slept, and dreamed of the Fleece of Gold.

Next morning the heroes awoke, and left the ship moored in the river's mouth, hidden by tall reeds, for they took down the mast, lest it should be seen. Then they walked toward the city of Colchis, and they passed through a strange and horrible wood. Dead men, bound together with cords, were hanging from the branches, for the Colchis people buried women, but hung dead men from the branches of trees. Then they came to the palace, where King Æêtes lived, with his young son Absyrtus, and his daughter Chalciope, who had been the wife of Phrixus, and his younger daughter, Medea, who was a witch, and the priestess of Brimo, a dreadful goddess. Now Chalciope came out and welcomed Jason, for she knew the heroes were of her dear husband's country. And beautiful Medea, the dark witch girl, came forth and saw Jason, and as soon as she saw him she loved him more than her father and her brother and all her father's house. For his bearing was gallant, and his armour golden, and long yellow hair fell over his shoulders, and over the leopard skin that he wore above his armour. Medea turned white and then red, and cast down her eyes, but Chalciope took the heroes to the baths, and gave them food, and they were brought to Æêtes, who asked them why they came, and they told him that they desired the Fleece of Gold, and he was very angry, and told them that only to a better man than himself would he give up that Fleece. If any wished to prove himself worthy of it he must tame two bulls which breathed flame from their nostrils, and must plough four acres with these bulls, and next he must sow the field with the teeth of a dragon, and these teeth when sown would immediately grow up into armed men. Jason said that, as it must be, he would try this adventure, but he went sadly enough back to the ship and did not notice how kindly Medea was looking after him as he went.

Now, in the dead of night, Medea could not sleep, because she was so sorry for the stranger, and she knew that she could help him by her magic. But she remembered how her father would burn her for a witch if she helped Jason, and a great shame, too, came on her that she should prefer a stranger to her own people. So she arose in the dark, and stole just as she was to her sister's room, a white figure roaming like a ghost in the palace. At her sister's door she turned back in shame, saying, 'No, I will never do it,' and she went back again to her chamber, and came again, and knew not what to do; but at last she returned to her own bower, and threw herself on her bed, and wept. Her sister heard her weeping, and came to her and they cried together, but softly, that no one might hear them. For Chalciope was as eager to help the Greeks for love of Phrixus, her dead husband, as Medea was for the love of Jason.

At last Medea promised to carry to the temple of the goddess of whom she was a priestess, a drug that would tame the bulls which dwelt in the field of that temple. But still she wept and wished that she were dead, and had a mind to slay herself; yet, all the time, she was longing for the dawn, that she might go and see Jason, and give him the drug, and see his face once more, if she was never to see him again. So, at dawn she bound up her hair, and bathed her face, and took the drug, which was pressed from a flower. That flower first blossomed when the eagle shed the blood of Prometheus on the earth. The virtue of the juice of the flower was this, that if a man anointed himself with it, he could not that day be wounded by swords, and fire could not burn him. So she placed it in a vial beneath her girdle, and she went with other girls, her friends, to the temple of the goddess. Now Jason had been warned by Chalciope to meet her there, and he was coming with Mopsus who knew the speech of birds. But Mopsus heard a crow that sat on a poplar tree speaking to another crow, saying:

'Here comes a silly prophet, and sillier than a goose. He is walking with a young man to meet a maid, and does not know that, while he is there to hear, the maid will not say a word that is in her heart. Go away, foolish prophet; it is not you she cares for.'

Then Mopsus smiled, and stopped where he was; but Jason went on, where Medea was pretending to play with the girls, her companions. When she saw Jason she felt as if she could neither go forward, nor go back, and she was very pale. But Jason told her not to be afraid, and asked her to help him, but for long she could not answer him; however, at the last, she gave him the drug, and taught him how to use it. 'So shall you carry the fleece to Iolcos, far away, but what is it to me where you go when you have gone from here? Still remember the name of me, Medea, as I shall remember you. And may there come to me some voice, or some bird bearing the message, whenever you have quite forgotten me.'

But Jason answered, 'Lady, let the winds blow what voice they will, and what that bird will, let him bring. But no wind or bird shall ever bear the news that I have forgotten you, if you will cross the sea with me, and be my wife.'

Then she was glad, and yet she was afraid, at the thought of that dark voyage, with a stranger, from her father's home and her own. So they parted, Jason to the ship, and Medea to the palace. But in the morning Jason anointed himself and his armour with the drug, and all the heroes struck at him with spears and swords, but the swords would not bite on him nor on his armour. He felt so strong and light that he leaped in the air with joy, and the sun shone on his glittering shield. Now they all went up together to the field where the bulls were breathing flame. There already was Æêtes, with Medea, and all the Colchians had come to see Jason die. A plough had been brought to which he was to harness the bulls. Then he walked up to them, and they blew fire at him that flamed all round him, but the magic drug protected him. He took a horn of one bull in his right hand, and a horn of the other in his left, and dashed their heads together so mightily that they fell.

When they rose, all trembling, he yoked them to the plough, and drove them with his spear, till all the field was ploughed in straight ridges and furrows. Then he dipped his helmet in the river, and drank water, for he was weary; and next he sowed the dragon's teeth on the right and left. Then you might see spear points, and sword points, and crests of helmets break up from the soil like shoots of corn, and presently the earth was shaken like sea waves, as armed men leaped out of the furrows, all furious for battle, and all rushed to slay Jason. But he, as Medea had told him to do, caught up a great rock, and threw it among them, and he who was struck by the rock said to his neighbour, 'You struck me; take that!' and ran his spear through that man's breast, but before he could draw it out another man had cleft his helmet with a stroke, and so it went: an hour of striking and shouting, while the sparks of fire sprang up from helmet and breastplate and shield. The furrows ran red with blood, and wounded men crawled on hands and knees to strike or stab those that were yet standing and fighting. So axes and sword and spear flashed and fell, till now all the men were down but one, taller and stronger than the rest. Round him he looked, and saw only Jason standing there, and he staggered toward him, bleeding, and lifting his great axe above his head. But Jason only stepped aside from the blow which would have cloven him to the waist, the last blow of the Men of the Dragon's Teeth, for he who struck fell, and there he lay and died.

Then Jason went to the king, where he sat looking darkly on, and said, 'O King, the field is ploughed, the seed is sown, the harvest is reaped. Give me now the Fleece of Gold, and let me be gone.' But the king said, 'Enough is done. To-morrow is a new day. To-morrow shall you win the Fleece.'

Then he looked sidewise at Medea, and she knew that he suspected her, and she was afraid.

Æêtes went and sat brooding over his wine with the captains of his people; and his mood was bitter, both for loss of the Fleece, and because Jason had won it not by his own prowess, but by the magic aid of Medea. As for Medea herself, it was the king's purpose to put her to a cruel death, and this she needed not her witchery to know, and a fire was in her eyes, and terrible sounds were ringing in her ears, and it seemed she had but two choices: to drink poison and die, or to flee with the heroes in the ship 'Argo.' But at last flight seemed better than death. So she hid all her engines of witchcraft in the folds of her gown, and she kissed her bed where she would never sleep again, and the posts of the door, and she caressed the very walls with her hand in that last farewell. And she cut a long lock of her yellow hair, and left it in the room, a keepsake to her mother dear, in memory of her maiden days. 'Good-bye, my mother,' she said, 'this long lock I leave thee in place of me; good-bye, a long good-bye, to me who am going on a long journey; good-bye, my sister Chalciope, good-bye! dear house, good-bye!'

Then she stole from the house, and the bolted doors leaped open at their own accord at the swift spell Medea murmured. With her bare feet she ran down the grassy paths, and the daisies looked black against the white feet of Medea. So she sped to the temple of the goddess, and the moon overhead looked down on her. Many a time had she darkened the moon's face with her magic song, and now the Lady Moon gazed white upon her, and said, 'I am not, then, the only one that wanders in the night for love, as I love Endymion the sleeper, who sleeps on the crest of the Latmian hill, and beholds me in his dreams. Many a time hast thou darkened my face with thy songs, and made night black with thy sorceries, and now thou too art in love! So go thy way, and bid thy heart endure, for a sore fate is before thee!'

But Medea hastened on till she came to the high river bank, and saw the heroes, merry at their wine in the light of a blazing fire. Thrice she called aloud, and they heard her, and came to her, and she said, 'Save me, my friends, for all is known, and my death is sure. And I will give you the Fleece of Gold for the price of my life.'

Then Jason swore that she should be his wife, and more dear to him than all the world. So she went aboard their boat, and swiftly they rowed up stream to the dark wood where the dragon who never sleeps lay guarding the Fleece of Gold. There she landed, and Jason, and Orpheus with his harp, and through the wood they went, but that old serpent saw them coming, and hissed so loud that women wakened in Colchis town, and children cried to their mothers. But Orpheus struck softly on his harp, and he sang a hymn to Sleep, bidding him come and cast a slumber on the dragon's wakeful eyes. This was the song he sang:

Sleep! King of Gods and men!
Come to my call again,
Swift over field and fen,
Mountain and deep:
Come, bid the waves be still;
Sleep, streams on height and hill;
Beasts, birds, and snakes, thy will
Conquereth, Sleep!
Come on thy golden wings,
Come ere the swallow sings,
Lulling all living things,

Fly they or creep!
Come with thy leaden wand,
Come with thy kindly hand,
Soothing on sea or land
Mortals that weep.
Come from the cloudy west,
Soft over brain and breast,
Bidding the Dragon rest,
Come to me, Sleep!

This was Orpheus's song, and he sang so
sweetly that the bright, small eyes of the dragon
closed, and all his hard coils softened and
uncurled. Then Jason set his foot on the dragon's
neck and hewed off his head, and lifted down the
Golden Fleece from the sacred oak tree, and it
shone like a golden cloud at dawn. He waited not
to wonder at it, but he and Medea and Orpheus
hurried through the wet wood-paths to the ship,
and threw it on board, cast a cloak over it, and
bade the heroes sit down to the oars, half of them,
but the others to take their shields and stand each
beside the oarsmen, to guard them from the
arrows of the Colchians. Then he cut the stern
cables with his sword, and softly they rowed, under
the bank, down the dark river to the sea. But the
hissing of the dragon had already awakened the

Colchians, and lights were flitting by the palace windows, and Æêtes was driving in his chariot with all his men down to the banks of the river. Then their arrows fell like hail about the ship, but they rebounded from the shields of the heroes, and the swift ship sped over the bar, and leaped as she felt the first waves of the salt sea.

And now the Fleece was won. But it was weary work bringing it home to Greece, and Medea and Jason did a deed which angered the gods. They slew her brother Absyrtus, who followed after them with a fleet, and cut him limb from limb, and when Æêtes came with his ships, and saw the dead limbs, he stopped, and went home, for his heart was broken. The gods would not let the Greeks return by the way they had come, but by strange ways where never another ship has sailed. Up the Ister (the Danube) they rowed, through countries of savage men, till the 'Agro' could go no farther, by reason of the narrowness of the stream. Then they hauled her overland, where no man knows, but they launched her on the Elbe at last, and out into a sea where never sail had been seen. Then they were driven wandering out into Ocean, and to a fairy, far-off isle where Lady Circe dwelt. Circe was the sister of King Æêtes, both were children of the Sun God, and Medea hoped that Circe would be kind to her, as she could not have heard of the slaying of Absyrtus. Medea and Jason went up through the woods of the isle to the house of Circe, and had no fear of the lions and wolves and bears that guarded the house. These knew that Medea was an enchantress, and they fawned on her and Jason and let them pass. But in the house they found Circe clad in dark mourning raiment, and all her long black hair fell wet and dripping to her feet, for she had seen visions of terror and sin, and therefore she had purified herself in salt water of the sea. The walls of her chamber, in the night, had shone as with fire, and dripped as with blood, and a voice of wailing had broken forth, and the spirit of dead Absyrtus had cried in her ears.

When Medea and Jason entered her hall, Circe bade them sit down, and called her bower maidens, fairies of woods and waters, to strew a table with a cloth of gold, and set on it food and wine. But Jason and Medea ran to the hearth, the sacred place of the house to which men that have done murder flee, and there they are safe, when they come in their flight to the house of a stranger. They cast ashes from the hearth on their heads, and Circe knew that they had slain Absyrtus. Yet she was of Medea's near kindred, and she respected the law of the hearth. Therefore she did the rite of purification, as was the custom, cleansing blood with blood, and she burned in the fire a cake of honey, and meal, and oil, to appease the Furies who revenge the deaths of kinsmen by the hands of kinsmen.

When all was done, Jason and Medea rose from their knees, and sat down on chairs in the hall, and Medea told Circe all her tale, except the slaying of Absyrtus.

'More and worse than you tell me you have done,' said Circe, 'but you are my brother's daughter.'

Then she advised them of all the dangers of their way home to Greece, how they must shun the Sirens, and Scylla and Charybdis, and she sent a messenger, Iris, the goddess of the Rainbow, to bid Thetis help them through the perils of the sea, and bring them safe to Phæacia, where the Phæacians would send them home.

'But you shall never be happy, nor know one good year in all your lives,' said Circe, and she bade them farewell.

They went by the way that Odysseus went on a later day; they passed through many perils, and came to Iolcos, where Pelias was old, and made Jason reign in his stead.

But Jason and Medea loved each other no longer, and many stories, all different from each other, are told concerning evil deeds that they wrought, and certainly they left each other, and Jason took another wife, and Medea went to Athens. Here she lived in the palace of Ægeus, an unhappy king who had been untrue to his own true love, and therefore the gods took from him courage and strength. But about Medea at Athens the story is told in the next tale, the tale of Theseus, Ægeus's son.

THESEUS AND THE CENTAUR

Now, as ancestors of the fifth and final generation of man, the ancient Greek heroes were often associated with specific city-states. They may have founded a kingdom or simply ruled there in the legendary past, but the Greeks in those provinces saw fit to pay particular homage to their memory. Theseus was one such hero to the Ancient Athenians. As an ancient king of Athens, Theseus was credited with countless impressive feats by the Athenian people; often he was even given credit for mythical deeds that were attributed to heroes like Heracles elsewhere in Greece. In the tale recounted by Gustav Schwab here, Theseus's good reputation earns him an invite to an illustrious wedding between the hero Pirithous and princess Hippodamia. Yet Theseus's strength and cunning are once again challenged when the half man, half horse race of centaurs disrupt the event, a common problem with centaurs in Greek myth.

Theseus, the hero king of Athens, had a reputation for great strength and bravery; but Pirithous, the son of Ixion, one of the most famous heroes of antiquity, wished to put him to the test. He therefore drove the cattle which belonged to Theseus away from Marathon, and when he heard that Theseus, weapon in hand, was following him, then, indeed, he had what he desired. He did not flee, but turned around to meet him.

When the two heroes were near enough to see each other, each was so filled with admiration for the beautiful form and the bravery of his opponent that, as if at a given signal, both threw down their weapons and hastened toward each other. Pirithous extended his hand to Theseus and proposed that the latter act as arbitrator for the settlement of the dispute about the cattle: whatever satisfaction Theseus would demand Pirithous would willingly give.

"The only satisfaction which I desire," answered Pirithous, "is that you instead of my enemy become my friend and comrade in arms."

Then the two heroes embraced each other and swore eternal friendship.

Soon after this Pirithous chose the Thessalian princess, Hippodamia, from the race of Lapithæ, for his bride, and invited Theseus to the wedding. The Lapithæ, among whom the ceremony took place, were a famous family of Thessalians, rugged mountaineers, in some respects resembling animals—the first mortals who had learned to manage a horse. But the bride, who had sprung from this race, was not at all like the men of her people. She was of noble form, with delicate, youthful face, so beautiful that all the guests praised Pirithous for his good fortune.

The assembled princes of Thessaly were at the wedding feast, and also the Centaurs, relatives of Pirithous. The Centaurs were half men, the offspring which a cloud, assuming the form of the goddess Hera, had born to Ixion, the father of Pirithous. They were the eternal enemies of the Lapithæ. Upon this occasion, however, and for the sake of the bride, they had forgotten past grudges and come together to the joyful celebration. The noble castle of Pirithous resounded with glad tumult; bridal songs were sung; wine and food abounded. Indeed, there were so many guests that the palace would not accommodate all. The

Lapithæ and Centaurs sat at a special table in a grotto shaded by trees.

For a long time the festivities went on with undisturbed happiness. Then the wine began to stir the heart of the wildest of the Centaurs, Eurytion, and the beauty of the Princess Hippodamia awoke in him the mad desire of robbing the bridegroom of his bride. Nobody knew how it came to pass; nobody noticed the beginning of the unthinkable act; but suddenly the guests saw the wild Eurytion lifting Hippodamia from her feet, while she struggled and cried for help. His deed was the signal for the rest of the drunken Centaurs to do likewise, and before the strange heroes and the Lapithæ could leave their places, every one of the Centaurs had roughly seized one of the Thessalian princesses who served at the court of the king or who had assembled as guests at the wedding.

The castle and the grotto resembled a besieged city; the cry of the women sounded far and wide. Quickly friends and relatives sprang from their places.

"What delusion is this, Eurytion," cried Theseus, "to vex Pirithous while I still live, and by so doing arouse the anger of two heroes?" With these words he forced his way through the crowd and tore the stolen bride from the struggling robber.

Eurytion said nothing, for he could not excuse his deed, but he lifted his hand toward Theseus and gave him a rough knock in the chest. Then Theseus, who had no weapon at hand, seized an iron jug of embossed workmanship which stood near by and flung it into the face of his opponent with such force that the Centaur fell backward on the ground, while brains and blood oozed from the wound in his head.

"To arms!" the cry arose from all sides. At first beakers, flasks and bowls flew back and forth. Then one sacrilegious monster grabbed the oblations from the neighboring apartments. Another tore down the lamp which burned over the table, while still another fought with a sacrificial deer which had hung on one side of the grotto. A frightful slaughter ensued. Rhoetus, the most wicked of the Centaurs after Eurytion, seized the largest brand from the altar and thrust it into the gaping wound of one of the fallen Lapithæ, so that the blood hissed like iron in a furnace. In opposition to him rose Dryas, the bravest of the Lapithæ, and seizing a glowing log from the fire, thrust it into the Centaur's neck. The fate of this Centaur atoned for the death of his fallen companion, and Dryas turned to the raging mob and laid five of them low.

Then the spear of the brave hero Pirithous flew

forth and pierced a mighty Centaur, Petraus, just as he was about to uproot a tree to use it for a club. The spear pinned him against the knotted oak. A second, Dictys, fell at the stroke of the Greek hero, and in falling snapped off a mighty ash tree; a third, wishing to avenge him, was crushed by Theseus with an oak club.

The most beautiful and youthful of the Centaurs was Cyllarus. His long hair and beard were golden; his smile was friendly; his neck, shoulders, hands and breast were as beautiful as if formed by an artist. Even the lower part of his body, the part which resembled a horse, was faultless, pitch-black in color, with legs and tail of lighter dye. He had come to the feast with his wife, the beautiful Centaur, Hylonome, who at the table had leaned gracefully against him and even now united with him in the raging fight. He received from an unknown hand a light wound near his heart, and sank dying in the arms of his wife. Hylonome nursed his dying form, kissed him and tried to retain the fleeting breath. When she saw that he was gone she drew a dagger from her breast and stabbed herself.

For a long time still the fight between the Lapithæ and the Centaurs continued, but at last night put an end to the tumult. Then Pirithous remained in undisturbed possession of his bride, and on the following morning Theseus departed, bidding farewell to his friend. The common fight had quickly welded the fresh tie of their brotherhood into an indestructible bond.

ICARUS

The story of Icarus has proven to be a timeless cautionary tale no matter what moral a particular generation may take away from it: listen to your parents; exercise caution; arrogance is dangerous; use your brain; the sun is really hot. It is easy amidst these messages to lose sympathy for our hero's plight. Jean Lang's retelling of this ancient myth turns back the clock to the time before Icarus donned his wings, however, and paints an emotional picture of a father and son imprisoned by a greedy king. Her version strays only from the original in having them locked in a tower instead of the labyrinth itself. Icarus in his reckless youth may forget to heed his father's warning, yet many heroes do far worse and come out unscathed. One momentary mistake, meanwhile, spells disaster for both Icarus and Daedalus in this tragic tale.

Fourteen years only have passed since our twentieth century began. In those fourteen years how
many a father's and mother's heart has bled for the
death of gallant sons, greatly-promising, greatly-
daring, who have sought to rule the skies? With
wings not well enough tried, they have soared
dauntlessly aloft, only to add more names to the
tragic list of those whose lives have been sacrificed
in order that the groping hands of science may
become sure, so that in time the sons of men may
sail through the heavens as fearlessly as their
fathers sailed through the seas.

High overhead we watch the monoplane, the
great, swooping thing, like a monster black-winged
bird, and our minds travel back to the story of
Icarus, who died so many years ago that there are
those who say that his story is but a foolish fable,
an idle myth.

Daedalus, grandson of a king of Athens, was the
greatest artificer of his day. Not only as an archi-
tect was he great, but as a sculptor he had the
creative power, not only to make men and women

and animals that looked alive, but to cause them to move and to be, to all appearances, endowed with life. To him the artificers who followed him owed the invention of the axe, the wedge, the wimble, and the carpenter's level, and his restless mind was ever busy with new inventions. To his nephew, Talus, or Perdrix, he taught all that he himself knew of all the mechanical arts. Soon it seemed that the nephew, though he might not excel his uncle, equalled Daedalus in his inventive power. As he walked by the seashore, the lad picked up the spine of a fish, and, having pondered its possibilities, he took it home, imitated it in iron, and so invented the saw. A still greater invention followed this. While those who had always thought that there could be none greater than Daedalus were still acclaiming the lad, there came to him the idea of putting two pieces of iron together, connecting them at one end with a rivet, and sharpening both ends, and a pair of compasses was made. Louder still were the acclamations of the people. Surely greater than Daedalus was here. Too much was this for the artist's jealous spirit.

One day they stood together on the top of the Acropolis, and Daedalus, murder that comes from jealousy in his heart, threw his nephew down. Down, down he fell, knowing well that he was going to meet a cruel death, but Pallas Athené, protectress of all clever craftsmen, came to his rescue. By her Perdrix was turned into the bird that still bears his name, and Daedalus beheld Perdrix, the partridge, rapidly winging his way to the far-off fields. Since then, no partridge has ever built or roosted in a high place, but has nestled in the hedge-roots and amongst the standing corn, and as we mark it we can see that its flight is always low.

For his crime Daedalus was banished from Athens, and in the court of Minos, king of Crete, he found a refuge. He put all his mighty powers at the service of Minos, and for him designed an intricate labyrinth which, like the river Meander, had neither beginning nor ending, but ever returned on itself in hopeless intricacy. Soon he stood high in the favour of the king, but, ever greedy for power, he incurred, by one of his daring inventions, the wrath of Minos. The angry monarch threw him into prison, and imprisoned along with him his son, Icarus. But prison bars and locks did not exist that were strong enough to baffle this master craftsman, and from the tower in which they were shut, Daedalus and his son were not long in making their escape. To escape from Crete was a less easy matter. There were many places in that wild island where it was easy for the father and son to hide, but the subjects of Minos were mostly mariners, and Daedalus knew well that all along the shore they kept watch lest he should make him a boat, hoist on it one of the sails of which he was part inventor, and speed away to safety like a sea-bird driven before the gale. Then did there come to Daedalus, the pioneer of inventions, the great idea that by his skill he might make a way for himself and his son through another element than water. And he laughed aloud in his hiding place amongst the cypresses on the hillside at the thought of how he would baffle the simple sailor-men who watched each creek and beach down on the shore. Mockingly, too, did he think of King Minos, who had dared to pit his power against the wits and skill of Daedalus, the mighty craftsman.

Many a Cretan bird was sacrificed before the task which the inventor had set himself was accomplished. In a shady forest on the mountains he fashioned light wooden frames and decked them with feathers, until at length they looked like the pinions of a great eagle, or of a swan that flaps its majestic way from lake to river. Each feather was bound on with wax, and the mechanism of the wings was so perfect a reproduction of that of the wings from which the feathers had been plucked, that on the first day that he fastened them to his back and spread them out, Daedalus found that he could fly even as the bird flew. Two pairs he made; having tested one pair, a second pair was made for Icarus, and, circling round him like a mother bird that teaches her nestlings how to fly, Daedalus, his heart big with the pride of invention, showed Icarus how he might best soar upwards to the sun or dive down to the blue sea far below, and how he might conquer the winds and the air currents of the sky and make them his servants.

That was a joyous day for father and son, for the father had never before drunk deeper of the intoxicating wine of the gods—Success—and for the lad it was all pure joy. Never before had he known freedom and power so utterly glorious. As a little child he had watched the birds fly far away over the blue hills to where the sun was setting, and had longed for wings that he might follow them in their flight. At times, in his dreams, he had known the power, and in his dreaming fancy had risen from the cumbering earth and soared high above the trees and fields on strong pinions that bore him away to the fair land of heart's desire—to the Islands of the Blessed. But when Sleep left him and the dreams silently slipped out before the coming of the light of day, and the boy sprang from his couch and eagerly spread his arms as, in his dreams, he had done, he could no longer fly. Disappointment and unsatisfied longing ever came with his waking hours. Now all that had come to an end, and Daedalus was glad and proud as well to watch his son's joy and his fearless daring. One word of counsel only did he give him.

"Beware, dear son of my heart," he said, "lest in thy new-found power thou seekest to soar even to the gates of Olympus. For as surely as the scorching rays from the burnished wheels of the chariot of Apollo smite thy wings, the wax that binds on thy feathers will melt, and then will come upon thee and on me woe unutterable."

In his dreams that night Icarus flew, and when he awoke, fearing to find only the haunting remembrance of a dream, he found his father standing by the side of his bed of soft leaves under the shadowy cypresses, ready to bind on his willing shoulders the great pinions that he had made.

Gentle Dawn, the rosy-fingered, was slowly making her way up from the East when Daedalus and Icarus began their flight. Slowly they went at first, and the goat-herds who tended their flocks on the slopes of Mount Ida looked up in fear when they saw the dark shadows of their way out to sea. From the river beds the waterfowl arose from the reeds, and with great outcry flew with all their swiftness to escape them. And down by the sea-shore the mariners' hearts sank within them as they watched, believing that a sight so strange must be a portent of disaster. Homewards they went in haste to offer sacrifices on the altars of Poseidon, ruler of the deep.

Samos and Delos were passed on the left and Lebynthos on the right, long ere the sun-god had started on his daily course, and as the mighty wings of Icarus cleft the cold air, the boy's slim body grew chilled, and he longed for the sun's rays to turn the waters of the Ægean Sea over which he flew from green-grey into limpid sapphire and emerald and burning gold. Towards Sicily he and his father bent their course, and when they saw the beautiful island afar off lying like a gem in the sea, Apollo made the waves in which it lay, for it a fit-ting setting. With a cry of joy Icarus marked the sun's rays paint the chill water, and Apollo looked down at the great white-winged bird, a snowy swan with the face and form of a beautiful boy, who sped exulting onwards, while a clumsier thing, with wings of darker hue, followed less quickly, in the same line of flight. As the god looked, the warmth that radiated from his chariot touched the icy limbs of Icarus as with the caressing touch of gentle, life-giving hands. Not long before, his flight had lagged a little, but now it seemed as if new life was his. Like a bird that wheels and soars and dives as if for lightness of heart, so did Icarus, until each feather of his plumage had a sheen of silver and of gold. Down, down, he darted, so near the water that almost the white-tipped waves caught at his wings as he skimmed over them. Then up, up, up he soared, ever higher, higher still, and when he saw the radiant sun-god smiling down on him, the warning of Daedalus was forgotten. As he had excelled other lads in foot races, now did Icarus wish to excel the birds themselves. Daedalus he left far behind, and still upwards he mounted. So strong he felt, so fearless was he, that to him it seemed that he could storm Olympus, that he could call to Apollo as he swept past him in his flight, and dare him to race for a wager from the Ægean Sea to where the sun-god's horses took their nightly rest by the trackless seas of the unknown West.

In terror his father watched him, and as he called to him in a voice of anguished warning that was drowned by the whistling rush of the air currents through the wings of Icarus and the moist whisper of the clouds as through them he cleft a way for himself, there befell the dreaded thing. It seemed as though the strong wings had begun to lose their power. Like a wounded bird Icarus fluttered, lunged sidewise from the straight, clean line of his flight, recovered himself, and fluttered again. And then, like the bird into whose soft breast the sure hand of a mighty archer has driven an arrow, downwards he fell, turning over and yet turning again, downwards, ever downwards, until he fell with a plunge into the sea that still was radiant in shining emerald and translucent blue.

Then did the car of Apollo drive on. His rays had slain one who was too greatly daring, and now they fondled the little white feathers that had fallen from the broken wings and floated on the water like the petals of a torn flower.

On the dead, still face of Icarus they shone, and they spangled as if with diamonds the wet plumage that still, widespread, bore him up on the waves.

Stricken at heart was Daedalus, but there was no time to lament his son's untimely end, for even now the black-prowed ships of Minos might be in pursuit. Onward he flew to safety, and in Sicily built a temple to Apollo, and there hung up his wings as a propitiatory offering to the god who had slain his son.

And when grey night came down on that part of the sea that bears the name of Icarus to this day, still there floated the body of the boy whose dreams had come true. For only a little while had he known the exquisite realisation of dreamed-of potentialities, for only a few hours tasted the sweetness of perfect pleasure, and then, by an over-daring flight, had lost it all for ever.

The sorrowing Nereids sang a dirge over him as he was swayed gently hither and thither by the tide, and when the silver stars came out from the dark firmament of heaven and were reflected in the blackness of the sea at night, it was as though a velvet pall, silver-decked in his honour, was spread around the slim white body with its outstretched snowy wings.

So much had he dared—so little accomplished.

Is it not the oft-told tale of those who have fol-lowed Icarus? Yet who can say that gallant youth has lived in vain when, as Icarus did, he has breasted the very skies, has flown with fearless heart and soul to the provinces of the deathless gods?—when, even for the space of a few of the heart-beats of Time, he has tasted supreme power—the ecstasy of illimitable happiness?

THE STORY OF ORPHEUS
AND EURYDICE

The myth of Orpheus and Eurydice is the quintes-
sential tragic love story. Orpheus was the son of
Apollo, the god of music himself, and the most
accomplished musician on earth. While he appears
in a number of Greek myths, including the voyage
of the Argo alongside Jason and his crew, it is the
story of his marriage to Eurydice which has continued to capture countless imaginations since its
inception. It has been adapted by medieval poets,
reimagined as ballets and operas, and depicted in
art from the renaissance to the art nouveau movement. Emilie Kip Baker's own retelling of this
myth captures the grief and heartbreak that runs
through its narrative, right down to the moment
we all want to shout through the page for Orpheus
to not turn around. So, put down your copy of
Romeo and Juliet and experience the original
doomed romantic tale.

The deeds of the immortal gods were told and sung at every fireside in Greece; and among these hero-tales there was none more popular than the story of how Apollo built for Neptune the famous wall of Troy. Many musicians would have been glad to perform a similar service for the mere fame that it would bring them, but they feared that the attempt to imitate Apollo would only result in failure and ridicule. So no mortal ever presumed to say that he could make rocks and stones obedient to the spell of his music. There was, however, one musician, Amphion, king of Thebes, who was anxious to prove that his playing was equal to Apollo's, but knowing how unwise it was to vie with an immortal, he determined not to test his skill publicly, but to carry out his cherished plan at night, when men were dreaming in their beds. He was eager to build a high wall around Thebes, and to build it as Apollo did the wall of Troy; so when the sun set, and darkness crept over the earth, Amphion stood just outside the city gates and began to play on his lyre. Immediately the stones rose from the ground and moved rhythmically into their places in the wall, which soon rose strong and high—a firmer defense than any that could be built by men's hands.

Another famous musician was Arion, who won not only praise for his great skill in playing, but also much wealth. Whenever a contest was held in which a prize of money was given, Arion was usually a competitor; and, as his music was really finer than that of most players, he easily won the reward. Once he was returning from a festival in Sicily whither many musicians had gone on account of the rich prize; and as he had come off victor, he was leaving the foreign shores well-laden with gold. Unfortunately he happened to embark on a ship owned by pirates who had heard of his great wealth, and were plotting to seize whatever part of it he had on board. As the easiest way to do this was to kill him, the pirates began to bind him with ropes that he might not be able to struggle when thrown overboard. Arion calmly accepted his fate, but begged the brutal crew to allow him to play once upon his lyre before going to his death. To this the pirates consented, and when the wonderful music filled the air, a school of dolphins swam toward the ship and kept close beside it, charmed by Arion's playing. Feeling sure that there was some magic in the music, the pirates hastened to throw the player and his lyre into the sea without waiting to bind him; but Arion did not drown as they had expected, for a friendly dolphin caught him on its back and swam with him to the shore, where he landed in safety. When in the course of time Arion died, the gods placed him, together with his lyre and the kindly dolphin, in the sky as constellations.

The most famous of all musicians, except the one who played in the shining halls of Olympus, was Orpheus, son of Apollo and of the muse Calliope. When he was a mere child, his father gave him a lyre and taught him to play upon it; but Orpheus needed very little instruction, for as soon as he laid his hand upon the strings the wild beasts crept out of their lairs to crouch beside him; the trees on the mountain-side moved nearer so that they might listen; and the flowers sprang up in clusters all around him, unwilling to remain any longer asleep in the earth.

When Orpheus sought in marriage the golden-haired Eurydice, there were other suitors for her hand, but though they brought rich gifts, gathered out of many lands, they could not win the maiden's love, and she turned from them to bestow her hand upon Orpheus who had no way to woo her but with his music. On the wedding day there was the usual mirth and feasting, but one event occurred that cast a gloom over the happiness of the newly-married pair. When Hymen, god of marriage, came with his torch to bless the nuptial feast, the light that should have burned clear and pure began to smoke ominously, as if predicting future disaster.

This evil omen was fulfilled all too soon, for one day when Eurydice was walking in the meadow, she met the youth Aristæus, who was so charmed with her beauty that he insisted upon staying beside her to pour his ardent speeches into her unwilling ears. To escape from these troublesome attentions, Eurydice started to run away, and as she ran she stepped on a poisonous snake, which quickly turned and bit her. She had barely time to reach her home before the poison had done its work, and Orpheus heard the sad story from her dying lips. As soon as Hermes had led away the soul of Eurydice, the bereaved husband hastened to the shining halls of Olympus, and throwing himself down before Zeus's golden throne, he implored that great ruler of gods and men to give him back his wife. There was always pity in the hearts of the gods for those who die in flowering time, so Zeus gave permission to Orpheus to go down into Hades, and beg of Hades the boon he craved.

It was a steep and perilous journey to the kingdom of the dead, and the road was one that no mortal foot had ever trod; but through his love for Eurydice Orpheus forgot the dangers of the way, and when he spoke her name, the terrors of the darkness vanished. In his hand he held his lyre, and when he arrived at the gate of Hades, where the fierce three-headed dog Cerberus refused to let him pass, Orpheus stood still in the uncertain darkness and began to play. And as he played the snarling of the dog ceased and the noise of its harsh breathing grew faint. Then Orpheus went on his way undisturbed, but still he played softly on his lyre, and the sounds floated far into the dismal interior of Hades, where the souls of the condemned labor forever at their tasks. Tantalus heard the music, and ceased to strive for a drop of the forbidden water; Ixion rested a moment beside his ever-revolving wheel; and Sisyphus stood listening, while the rock which he must roll through all eternity fell from his wearied arms. The daughters of Danaüs laid down their urns beside the sieve into which they were forever pouring water, and as the mournful wailing of Orpheus's lyre told the story of his lost love, they wept then for a sorrow not their own. So plaintive, indeed, was the music, that all the shadowy forms that flitted endlessly by shed tears of sympathy for the player's grief, and even the cheeks of the Furies were wet.

When Orpheus came before the throne of Hades, that relentless monarch repulsed him angrily as he attempted to plead his cause, and commanded him to depart. Then the son of Apollo began to play upon his lyre, and through his music he told the story of his loss, and besought the ruler of these myriad souls to give him the single one he craved. So wonderfully did Orpheus play that the hard heart of Hades was touched with pity, and he consented to restore Eurydice to her husband on condition that as they went out together from the loathed country of the dead he should not once turn his head to look upon her. To this strange decree Orpheus gladly promised obedience; so Eurydice was summoned from among the million shadow-shapes that throng the silent halls of death. Hades told her the condition on which her freedom was to be won, and then bade her follow her husband.

During all the wearisome journey back to earth, Orpheus never forgot the promise he had made, though he often longed to give just a hurried glance at the face of Eurydice to see whether it had lost its sadness. As they neared the spot where the first faint glimmerings of light filtered down into the impenetrable darkness, Orpheus thought he heard his wife calling, and he looked quickly around to find whether she was still following him. At that moment the slight form close behind him began to fade away, and a mournful voice—seemingly far in the distance—called to him a sad farewell.

He knew that no second chance would be given him to win his wife from Hades's hold, even if he could again charm the three-headed Cerberus or persuade Charon, the grim ferryman, to take him across the river. So he went forlornly back to earth and lived in a forest cave far from the companionship of men. At first there was only his lyre to share his solitude, but soon the forest creatures came to live beside him, and often sat listening to his music, looking exceedingly wise and sorrowful. Even in his sleepless hours, when he fancied he heard Eurydice calling, he was never quite alone, for the bat and owl and the things that love the darkness flitted about him, and he saw the glow-worms creep toward him out of the night-cold grass.

One day a party of Bacchantes found him seated outside the cave, playing the mournful music that told of his lost love, and they bade him change the sad notes to something gay so that they might dance. But Orpheus was too wrapped up in his sorrow to play any strain of cheerful music, and he refused to do as they asked. The Bacchantes were half maddened by their festival days of drinking, and this refusal so enraged them that they fell upon the luckless musician and tore him to pieces. Then they threw his mangled body into the river, and as the head of Orpheus drifted down the stream, his lips murmured again and again "Eurydice," until the hills echoed the beloved name, and the rocks and trees and rivers repeated it in mournful chorus. Later on, the Muses gathered up his remains to give them honorable burial; and it is said that over Orpheus's grave the nightingale sings more sweetly than in any other spot in Greece.

CIRCE'S PALACE

While titled Circe's Palace, this tale technically centres on the hero Odysseus, for whom Circe is both friend and foe. The narrative which Nathaniel Hawthorne retells here is but one incident within a much longer tale, one that traverses seas and continents, and lasts more than twenty years. The Greek king of Ithaca, Odysseus, is on his way home from fighting in the Trojan War. However, his reunion with both wife and son is delayed time and time again, due to various ill-fated encounters with the gods and creatures of Greek mythology. Despite this, the tale of Odysseus's shipwreck on a strange island with only one inhabitant manages to stand alone thanks to Hawthorne's immersive prose. And for those who remain curious about what comes before and after Odysseus's time on Circe's Island, you need look no further than Homer's *Odyssey*. Don't be surprised, however, if Hawthorne's chatty bird is missing.

"Who knows not Circe,
The daughter of the Sun, whose charmèd cup
Whoever tasted lost his upright shape,
And downward fell into a grovelling swine?"
Milton, *Comus*, 50–53.

Some of you have heard, no doubt, of the wise King Odysseus, and how he went to the siege of Troy, and how, after that famous city was taken and burned, he spent ten long years in trying to get back again to his own little kingdom of Ithaca. At one time, in the course of this weary voyage, he arrived at an island that looked very green and pleasant, but the name of which was unknown to him. For, only a little while before he came thither, he had met with a terrible hurricane, or rather a great many hurricanes at once, which drove his fleet of vessels into a strange part of the sea, where neither himself nor any of his mariners had ever sailed. This misfortune was entirely owing to the foolish curiosity of his shipmates, who, while Odysseus lay asleep, had untied some very bulky leathern bags, in which they supposed a valuable treasure to be concealed. But in each of these stout bags King Æolus, the ruler of the winds, had tied up a tempest, and had given it to Odysseus to keep, in order that he might be sure of a favourable passage homeward to Ithaca; and when the strings were loosened, forth rushed the whistling blasts, like air out of a blown bladder, whitening the sea with foam, and scattering the vessels nobody could tell whither.

Immediately after escaping from this peril, a still greater one had befallen him. Scudding before the hurricane, he reached a place which, as he afterwards found, was called Læstrygonia, where some monstrous giants had eaten up many of his companions, and had sunk every one of his vessels, except that in which he himself sailed, by flinging great masses of rock at them from the cliffs along the shore. After going through such troubles as these, you cannot wonder that King Odysseus was glad to moor his tempest-beaten bark in a quiet cove of the green island which I began with telling you about. But he had encountered so many dangers from giants, and one-eyed Cyclops, and monsters of the sea and land, that he could not help dreading some mischief, even in this pleasant and seemingly solitary spot. For two days, therefore, the poor weather-worn voyagers kept quiet, and either stayed on board of their vessel, or merely crept along under the cliffs that bordered the shore; and, to keep themselves alive, they dug shell-fish out of the sand, and sought for any little rill of fresh water that might be running towards the sea.

Before the two days were spent, they grew very weary of this kind of life; for the followers of King Odysseus, as you will find it important to remember, were terrible gormandizers, and pretty sure to grumble if they missed their regular meals, and their irregular ones besides. Their stock of provisions was quite exhausted, and even the shell-fish began to get scarce, so that they had now to choose between starving to death or venturing into the interior of the island, where perhaps some huge three-headed dragon or other horrible monster had his den. Such misshapen creatures were very numerous in those days, and nobody ever expected to make a voyage or take a journey without running more or less risk of being devoured by them.

But King Odysseus was a bold man as well as a prudent one; and on the third morning he determined to discover what sort of a place the island was, and whether it were possible to obtain a supply of food for the hungry mouths of his companions. So, taking a spear in his hand, he clambered to the summit of the cliff, and gazed round about him. At a distance, towards the centre of the island, he beheld the stately towers of what seemed to be a palace, built of snow-white marble, and rising in the midst of a grove of lofty trees. The thick branches of these trees stretched across the front of the edifice and more than half concealed it, although, from the portion which he saw, Odysseus judged it to be spacious and exceedingly beautiful, and probably the residence of some great nobleman or prince. A blue smoke went curling up from the chimney, and was almost the pleasantest part of the spectacle to Odysseus; for, from the abundance of this smoke, it was reasonable to conclude that there was a good fire in the kitchen, and that at dinner-time a plentiful banquet would be served up to the inhabitants of the palace, and to whatever guests might happen to drop in.

With so agreeable a prospect before him, Odysseus fancied that he could not do better than to go straight to the palace gate, and tell the master of it that there was a crew of poor shipwrecked mariners not far off, who had eaten nothing for a day or two, save a few clams and oysters, and would therefore be thankful for a little food. And the prince or nobleman must be a very stingy curmudgeon, to be sure, if at least, when his own dinner was over, he would not bid them welcome to the broken victuals from the table.

Pleasing himself with this idea, King Odysseus had made a few steps in the direction of the palace, when there was a great twittering and chirping from the branch of a neighbouring tree. A moment afterwards a bird came flying towards him, and hovered in the air, so as almost to brush his face with its wings. It was a very pretty little bird, with purple wings and body, and yellow legs, and a circle of golden feathers round its neck, and on its head a golden tuft, which looked like a king's crown in miniature. Odysseus tried to catch the bird, but it fluttered nimbly out of his reach, still chirping in a piteous tone, as if it could have told a lamentable story had it only been gifted with human language. And when he attempted to drive it away, the bird flew no farther than the bough of the next tree, and again came fluttering about his head, with its doleful chirp, as soon as he showed a purpose of going forward.

"Have you anything to tell me, little bird?" asked Odysseus.

And he was ready to listen attentively to whatever the bird might communicate; for, at the siege of Troy and elsewhere, he had known such odd things to happen that he would not have considered

it much out of the common run had this little feathered creature talked as plainly as himself.

"Peep!" said the bird, "peep, peep, pe-weep!"
And nothing else would it say, but only "Peep,
peep, pe-weep!" in a melancholy cadence, and over
and over and over again. As often as Odysseus
moved forward, however, the bird showed the
greatest alarm, and did its best to drive him back,
with the anxious flutter of its purple wings. Its
unaccountable behaviour made him conclude, at
last, that the bird knew of some danger that
awaited him, and which must needs be very terrible, beyond all question, since it moved even a
little fowl to feel compassion for a human being.
So he resolved for the present to return to the
vessel, and tell his companions what he had seen.

This appeared to satisfy the bird. As soon as
Odysseus turned back, it ran up the trunk of a tree,
and began to pick insects out of the bark with its
long, sharp bill; for it was a kind of woodpecker,
you must know, and had to get its living in the same
manner as other birds of that species. But every
little while, as it pecked at the bark of the tree, the
purple bird bethought itself of some secret sorrow,
and repeated its plaintive note of "Peep, peep, pe-
weep!"

On his way to the shore, Odysseus had the good

luck to kill a large stag, by thrusting his spear into its back. Taking it on his shoulders (for he was a remarkably strong man), he lugged it along with him, and flung it down before his hungry companions. I have already hinted to you what gormandizers some of the comrades of King Odysseus were. From what is related of them, I reckon that their favourite diet was pork, and that they had lived upon it until a good part of their physical substance was swine's flesh, and their tempers and dispositions were very much akin to the hog. A dish of venison, however, was no unacceptable meal to them, especially after feeding so long on oysters and clams. So, beholding the dead stag, they felt its ribs in a knowing way, and lost no time in kindling a fire of drift-wood to cook it. The rest of the day was spent in feasting, and if these enormous eaters got up from table at sunset it was only because they could not scrape another morsel off the poor animal's bones.

The next morning their appetites were as sharp as ever. They looked at Odysseus as if they expected him to clamber up the cliff again, and come back with another fat deer upon his shoulders. Instead of setting out, however, he summoned the whole crew together, and told them it was in vain to hope that he could kill a stag every day for their dinner, and therefore it was advisable to think of some other mode of satisfying their hunger.

"Now," said he, "when I was on the cliff yesterday, I discovered that this island is inhabited. At a considerable distance from the shore stood a marble palace, which appeared to be very spacious, and had a great deal of smoke curling out of one of its chimneys."

"Aha!" muttered some of his companions, smacking their lips. "That smoke must have come from the kitchen fire. There was a good dinner on the spit; and no doubt there will be as good a one today."

"But," continued the wise Odysseus, "you must remember, my good friends, our misadventure in the cavern of one-eyed Polyphemus, the Cyclops! Instead of his ordinary milk diet, did he not eat up two of our comrades for his supper, and a couple more for breakfast, and two at his supper again! Methinks I see him yet, the hideous monster, scanning us with that great red eye in the middle of his forehead, to single out the fattest. And then again, only a few days ago, did we not fall into the hands of the king of the Læstrygons, and those other horrible giants, his subjects, who devoured a great many more of us than are now left? To tell you the truth, if we go to yonder palace, there can be no question that we shall make our appearance at the dinner-table; but whether seated as guests, or served up as a food, is a point to be seriously considered."

"Either way," murmured some of the hungriest of the crew, "it will be better than starvation—particularly if one could be sure of being well fattened beforehand, and daintily cooked afterwards."

"That is a matter of taste," said King Odysseus, "and, for my own part, neither the most careful fattening nor the daintiest of cookery would reconcile me to being dished at last. My proposal is, therefore, that we divide ourselves into two equal parties, and ascertain, by drawing lots, which of the two shall go to the palace and beg for food and assistance. If these can be obtained, all is well. If not, and if the inhabitants prove as inhospitable as Polyphemus, or the Læstrygons, then there will but half of us perish, and the remainder may set sail and escape."

As nobody objected to this scheme, Odysseus proceeded to count the whole band, and found that there were forty-six men, including himself. He then numbered off twenty-two of them, and put Eurylochus (who was one of his chief officers, and second only to himself in sagacity) at their head. Odysseus took command of the remaining twenty-two men in person. Then, taking off his helmet, he put two shells into it, on one of which was written "Go", and on the other "Stay". Another person now held the helmet, while Odysseus and Eurylochus drew out each a shell; and the word "Go" was found written on that which Eurylochus had drawn. In this manner it was decided that Odysseus and his twenty-two men were to remain at the seaside until the other party should have found out what sort of treatment they might expect at the mysterious place. As there was no help for it, Eurylochus immediately set forth at the head of his twenty-two followers, who went off in a very melancholy state of mind, leaving their friends in hardly better spirits than themselves.

No sooner had they clambered up the cliff than they discerned the tall marble towers of the palace, ascending, as white as snow, out of the lovely green shadow of the trees which surrounded it. A gush of smoke came from a chimney in the rear of the edifice. This vapour rose high in the air, and, meeting with the breeze, was wafted seaward, and made to pass over the heads of the hungry mariners. When people's appetites are keen, they have a very quick scent for anything savoury in the wind.

"That smoke comes from the kitchen!" cried one of them, turning up his nose as high as he could, and snuffing eagerly. "And as sure as I'm a half-starved vagabond, I smell roast meat in it."

"Pig, roast pig!" said another. "Ah, the dainty little porker! My mouth waters for him!"

"Let us make haste," cried the others, "or we shall be too late for the good cheer!"

But scarcely had they made half a dozen steps from the edge of the cliff when a bird came fluttering to meet them. It was the same pretty little bird, with the purple wings and body, the yellow legs, the golden collar round its neck, and the crown-like tuft upon its head, whose behaviour had so much surprised Odysseus. It hovered about Eurylochus, and almost brushed his face with its wings.

"Peep, peep, pe—weep!" chirped the bird.

So plaintively intelligent was the sound that it seemed as if the little creature were going to break its heart with some mighty secret that it had to tell, and only this one poor note to tell it with.

"My pretty bird," said Eurylochus, for he was a wary person, and let no token of harm escape his notice, "my pretty bird, who sent you hither? And what is the message which you bring?"

"Peep, peep, pe—weep!" replied the bird very sorrowfully.

Then it flew towards the edge of the cliff and looked round at them, as if exceedingly anxious that they should return whence they came. Eurylochus and a few of the others were inclined to turn back. They could not help suspecting that the purple bird must be aware of something mischievous that would befall them at the palace, and the knowledge of which affected its airy spirit with a human sympathy and sorrow. But the rest of the voyagers, snuffing up the smoke from the palace kitchen, ridiculed the idea of returning to the vessel. One of them (more brutal than his fellows, and the most notorious gormandizer in the whole crew) said such a cruel and wicked thing that I wonder the mere thought did not turn him into a wild beast in shape, as he already was in his nature.

"This troublesome and impertinent little fowl!" said he, "would make a delicate titbit to begin dinner with. Just one plump morsel, melting away between the teeth. If he comes within my reach I'll catch him, and give him to the palace cook to be roasted on a skewer."

The words were hardly out of his mouth before the purple bird flew away, crying "Peep, peep, pe—weep!" more dolorously than ever.

"That bird," remarked Eurylochus, "knows more than we do about what awaits us at the palace."

"Come on, then," cried his comrades, "and we'll soon know as much as he does."

The party accordingly went onward through the green and pleasant wood. Every little while they caught new glimpses of the marble palace, which looked more and more beautiful the nearer they approached it.

So they hastened their steps towards the portal, but had not got half-way across the wide lawn when a pack of lions, tigers, and wolves came bounding to meet them. The terrified mariners started back, expecting no better fate than to be torn to pieces and devoured. To their surprise and joy, however, these wild beasts merely capered around them, wagging their tails, offering their heads to be stroked and patted, and behaving just like so many well-bred house-dogs when they wish to express their delight at meeting their master or their master's friends. The biggest lion licked the feet of Eurylochus, and every other lion, and every wolf and tiger, singled out one of his two-and-twenty followers, whom the beast fondled as if he loved him better than a beef-bone.

But for all that Eurylochus imagined that he saw something fierce and savage in their eyes; nor would he have been surprised at any moment to feel the big lion's terrible claws, or to see each of the tigers make a deadly spring, or each wolf leap at the throat of the man whom he had fondled. Their mildness seemed unreal, and a mere freak; but their savage nature was as true as their teeth and claws.

Nevertheless the men went safely across the lawn, with the wild beasts frisking about them, and doing no manner of harm; although, as they mounted the steps of the palace, you might possibly have heard a low growl, particularly from the wolves, as if they thought it a pity, after all, to let the strangers pass without so much as tasting what they were made of.

Eurylochus and his followers now passed under a lofty portal, and looked through the open doorway into the interior of the palace. The first thing that they saw was a spacious hall, and a fountain in the middle of it gushing up towards the ceiling out of a marble basin, and falling back into it with a continual plash. The water of this fountain, as it spouted upward, was constantly taking new shapes, not very distinctly, but plainly enough for a nimble fancy to recognize what they were. Now it was the shape of a man in a long robe, the fleecy whiteness of which was made out of the fountain's spray; now it was a lion, or a tiger, or a wolf, or an ass, or, as often as anything else, a hog wallowing in the marble basin as if it were his sty. It was either magic or some very curious machinery that caused the gushing waterspout to assume all these forms. But before the strangers had time to look closely at this wonderful sight, their attention was drawn off by a very sweet and agreeable sound. A woman's voice was singing melodiously in another room of the palace, and with her voice was mingled the noise of a loom, at which she was probably seated weaving a rich texture of cloth, and intertwining the high and low sweetness of her voice into a rich tissue of harmony.

By and by the song came to an end, and then all at once there were several feminine voices talking airily and cheerfully, with now and then a merry burst of laughter, such as you may always hear when three or four young women sit at work together.

"What a sweet song that was!" exclaimed one of the voyagers.

"Too sweet, indeed," answered Eurylochus, shaking his head. "Yet it was not so sweet as the song of the Sirens, those birdlike damsels who wanted to tempt us on the rocks, so that our vessel might be wrecked and our bones left whitening along the shore."

No warning or persuasion, however, had any effect on his companions. They went up to a pair of folding-doors at the farther end of the hall, and, throwing them wide open, passed into the next room. Eurylochus meanwhile had stepped behind a pillar. In the short moment while the folding-doors opened and closed again, he caught a glimpse of a very beautiful woman rising from the loom, and coming to meet the poor, weather-beaten wanderers, with a hospitable smile, and her hand stretched out in welcome. There were four other young women, who joined their hands and danced merrily forward, making gestures of obeisance to the strangers. They were only less beautiful than the lady who seemed to be their mistress. Yet Eurylochus fancied that one of them had sea-green hair, and that the close-fitting bodice of a second looked like the bark of a tree, and that both the others had something odd in their aspect, although he could not quite determine what it was in the little while that he had to examine them.

The folding-doors swung quickly back and left him standing behind the pillar, in the solitude of the outer hall. There Eurylochus waited until he was quite weary, and listened eagerly to every sound, but without hearing anything that could help him to guess what had become of his friends. Footsteps, it is true, seemed to be passing and repassing in other parts of the palace. Then there was a clatter of silver dishes, or golden ones, which made him imagine a rich feast in a splendid banqueting-hall. But by and by he heard a tremendous grunting and squealing, and then a sudden scampering, like that of small, hard hoofs over a marble floor, while the voices of the mistress and her four handmaidens were screaming all together in tones of anger and derision. Eurylochus could not conceive what had happened, unless a drove of swine had broken into the palace, attracted by the smell of the feast. Chancing to cast his eyes at the fountain, he saw that it did not shift its shape, as formerly, nor looked either like a long-robed man, or a lion, a tiger, a wolf, or an ass. It looked like nothing but a hog, which lay wallowing in the marble basin, and filled it from brim to brim.

But we must leave the prudent Eurylochus waiting in the outer hall, and follow his friends into the inner secrecy of the palace. As soon as the beautiful woman saw them, she arose from the loom, as I have told you, and came forward smiling and stretching out her hand. She took the hand of the foremost among them, and bade him and the whole party welcome.

"You have been long expected, my good friends," said she. "I desire to make you happy for as long a time as you may remain with me. For this purpose, my honoured guests, I have ordered a banquet to be prepared. Fish, fowl, and flesh, roasted and in luscious stews, and seasoned, I trust to all your tastes, are ready to be served up. If your appetites tell you it is dinner-time, then come with me to the festal saloon."

The beautiful woman now clapped her hands, and immediately there entered a train of two-and-twenty serving-men, bringing dishes of the richest food, all hot from the kitchen fire, and sending up such a steam that it hung like a cloud below the crystal dome of the saloon. An equal number of attendants brought great flagons of wine of various kinds, some of which sparkled as it was poured out, and went bubbling down the throat; while of other sorts the purple liquor was so clear that you could see the wrought figures at the bottom of the goblet. While the servants supplied the two-and-twenty guests with food and drink, the hostess and her four maidens went from one throne to another, exhorting them to eat their fill, and to quaff wine abundantly, and thus to recompense themselves, at this one banquet, for the many days when they had gone without a dinner. But whenever the mariners were not looking at them (which was pretty often, as they looked chiefly into the basins and platters), the beautiful woman and her damsels turned aside and laughed. Even the servants, as they knelt down to present the dishes, might be seen to grin and sneer while the guests were helping themselves to the offered dainties.

And once in a while the strangers seemed to taste something that they did not like.

"Here is an odd kind of a spice in this dish," said one. "I can't say it quite suits my palate. Down it goes, however."

"Send a good draught of wine down your throat," said his comrade on the next throne. "That is the stuff to make this sort of cookery relish well. Though I must needs say the wine has a queer taste too. But the more I drink of it the better I like the flavour."

Whatever little fault they might find with the dishes, they sat at dinner a prodigiously long while, and it would really have made you ashamed to see how they swilled down the liquor and gobbled up the food. They sat on golden thrones, to be sure, but they behaved like pigs in a sty, and if they had had their wits about them they might have guessed that this was the opinion of their beautiful hostess and her maidens. It brings a blush into my face to reckon up, in my own mind, what mountains of meat and pudding, and what gallons of wine these two-and-twenty guzzlers and gormandizers ate and drank. They forgot all about their homes, and their wives and children, and all about Odysseus, and everything else, except this banquet, at which they wanted to keep feasting for ever. But at length they began to give over, from mere incapacity to hold any more.

"That last bit of fat is too much for me," said one.

"And I have not room for another morsel," said his next neighbour, heaving a sigh. "What a pity! My appetite is as sharp as ever."

In short, they all left off eating, and leaned back on their thrones with such a stupid and helpless aspect as made them ridiculous to behold. When their hostess saw this, she laughed aloud; so did her four damsels; so did the two-and-twenty serving-men that bore the dishes, and their two-and-twenty fellows that poured out the wine. And the louder they all laughed, the more stupid and helpless did the two-and-twenty gormandizers look. Then the beautiful woman took her stand in the middle of the saloon, and, stretching out a slender rod (it had been all the while in her hand, although they never noticed it till this moment), she turned it from one guest to another, until each had felt it pointed at himself. Beautiful as her face was, and though there was a smile on it, it looked just as wicked and mischievous as the ugliest serpent that ever was seen; and fat-witted as the voyagers had made themselves, they began to suspect that they had fallen into the power of an evil-minded enchantress.

"Wretches," cried she, "you have abused a lady's hospitality, and in this princely saloon your behaviour has been suited to a hog-pen. You are already swine in everything but the human form, which you disgrace, and which I myself should be ashamed to keep a moment longer were you to share it with me. Assume your proper shapes, gormandizers, and begone to the sty!"

But, brutes as they certainly were, they yet had enough of human nature in them to be shocked at their own hideousness; and they uttered a vile grunt and squeal. So harsh and ear-piercing it was that you would have fancied a butcher was sticking his knife into each of their throats; or, at the very least, that somebody was pulling every hog by his funny little twist of a tail.

"Begone to your sty!" cried the enchantress, giving them some smart strokes with her wand, and then she turned to the serving-men. "Drive out these swines, and throw down some acorns for them to eat."

Meantime, as I told you before, Eurylochus had waited, and waited, and waited in the entrance-hall of the palace without being able to comprehend what had befallen his friends. At last, when the swinish uproar resounded through the palace, and when he saw the image of a hog in the marble basin, he thought it best to hasten back to the vessel and inform the wise Odysseus of these marvellous occurrences. So he ran as fast as he could down the steps, and never stopped to draw breath till he reached the shore.

"Why do you come alone?" asked King Odysseus, as soon as he saw him. "Where are your two-and-twenty comrades?"

At these questions Eurylochus burst into tears.

"Alas!" cried he, "I greatly fear that we shall never see one of their faces again."

Then he told Odysseus all that had happened as far as he knew it, and added that he suspected the beautiful woman to be a vile enchantress, and the marble palace, magnificent as it looked, to be only a dismal cavern in reality. As for his companions, he could not imagine what had become of them, unless they had been given to the swine to be devoured alive. At this intelligence all the voyagers were greatly affrighted. But Odysseus lost no time in girding on his sword, and hanging his bow and quiver over his shoulders, and taking a spear in his right hand. When his followers saw their wise leader making these preparations, they inquired whither he was going, and earnestly besought him not to leave them.

Had his followers dared, they would have detained him by force. But King Odysseus frowned sternly on them, and shook his spear, and bade them stop him at their peril. Seeing him so determined, they let him go, and sat down on the sand, as disconsolate a set of people as could be, waiting and praying for his return.

It happened to Odysseus, just as before, that when he had gone a few steps from the edge of the cliff, the purple bird came fluttering towards him, crying, "Peep, peep, pe-weep!" and using all the art it could to persuade him to go no farther.

"What mean you, little bird?" cried Odysseus. "You are arrayed like a king, in purple and gold, and wear a golden crown upon your head. Is it because I too am a king that you desire so earnestly to speak with me? If you can talk in human language, say what you would have me do."

"Peep!" answered the purple bird very dolorously. "Peep, peep, pe—we—ep!"

Certainly there lay some heavy anguish at the little bird's heart, and it was a sorrowful predicament that he could not at least have the consolation of telling what it was. But Odysseus had no time to waste in trying to get at the mystery. He therefore quickened his pace, and had gone a good way along the pleasant wood-path, when there met him a young man of very brisk and intelligent aspect, and clad in a rather singular garb. He wore a short cloak, and a sort of cap that seemed to be furnished with a pair of wings; and, from the lightness of his step, you would have supposed that there might likewise be wings on his feet. To enable him to walk still better (for he was always on one journey or another), he carried a winged staff, around which two serpents were wriggling and twisting. In short, I have said enough to make you guess that it was Quicksilver, and Odysseus (who knew him of old, and had learned a great deal of his wisdom from him) recognized him in a moment.

"Whither are you going in such a hurry, wise Odysseus?" asked Quicksilver. "Do you not know that this island is enchanted? The wicked enchantress (whose name is Circe, the sister of King Æetes) dwells in the marble palace which you see yonder among the trees. By her magic arts she changes every human being into the brute, beast, or fowl whom he happens most to resemble."

"That little bird which I met at the edge of the cliff," exclaimed Odysseus, "was he a human being once?"

"Yes," answered Quicksilver. "He was once a king named Picus, and a pretty good sort of a king too, only rather too proud of his purple robe, and his crown, and the golden chain about his neck; so he was forced to take the shape of a gaudy-feathered bird. The lions and wolves and tigers who will come running to meet you in front of the palace were formerly fierce and cruel men, resembling in their dispositions the wild beasts whose forms they now rightfully wear."

"And my poor companions," said Odysseus, "have they undergone a similar change through the arts of this wicked Circe?"

"You well know what gormandizers they were," replied Quicksilver—and, rogue that he was, he could not help laughing at the joke—"so you will not be surprised to hear that they have all taken the shapes of swine! If Circe had never done anything worse, I really should not think her so very much to blame."

"But can I do nothing to help them?" inquired Odysseus.

"It will require all your wisdom," said Quicksilver, "and a little of my own into the bargain, to keep your royal and sagacious self from being transformed into a fox. But do as I bid you, and the matter may end better than it has begun."

While he was speaking, Quicksilver seemed to be in search of something; he went stooping along the ground, and soon laid his hand on a little plant with a snow-white flower, which he plucked and smelt. Odysseus had been looking at that very spot only just before, and it appeared to him that the plant had burst into full flower the instant when Quicksilver touched it with his fingers.

"Take this flower, King Odysseus," said he. "Guard it as you do your eyesight; for I can assure you it is exceedingly rare and precious, and you might seek the whole earth over without ever finding another like it. Keep it in your hand, and smell of it frequently after you enter the palace, and while you are talking with the enchantress. Especially when she offers you food, or a draught of wine out of her goblet, be careful to fill your nostrils with the flower's fragrance. Follow these directions and you may defy her magic arts to change you into a fox."

Quicksilver then gave him some further advice how to behave, and, bidding him be bold and prudent, again assured him that, powerful as Circe was, he would have a fair prospect of coming safely out of her enchanted palace. After listening attentively, Odysseus thanked his good friend, and resumed his way. But he had taken only a few steps when, recollecting some other questions which he wished to ask, he turned round again, and beheld nobody on the spot where Quicksilver had stood; for that winged cap of his, and those winged shoes, with the help of the winged staff, had carried him quickly out of sight.

When Odysseus reached the lawn in front of the palace the lions and other savage animals came bounding to meet him, and would have fawned upon him and licked his feet. But the wise king struck at them with his long spear, and sternly bade them begone out of his path, for he knew that they had once been bloodthirsty men, and would now tear him limb from limb, instead of fawning upon him, could they do the mischief that was in their hearts. The wild beasts yelped and glared at him, and stood at a distance while he ascended the palace steps.

The king likewise heard the noise of the shuttle in the loom, and the sweet melody of the beautiful woman's song, and then the pleasant voices of herself and the four maidens talking together, with peals of merry laughter intermixed. But Odysseus did not waste much time in listening to the laughter or the song. He leaned his spear against one of the pillars of the hall, and then, after loosening his sword in the scabbard, stepped boldly forward and threw the folding-doors wide open. The moment she beheld his stately figure standing in the doorway, the beautiful woman rose from the loom and ran to meet him, with a glad smile throwing its sunshine over her face, and both her hands extended.

"Welcome, brave stranger!" cried she. "We were expecting you."

"Your companions," said she, "have already been received into my palace, and have enjoyed the hospitable treatment to which the propriety of their behaviour so well entitles them. If such be your pleasure, you shall first take some refreshment, and then join them in the elegant apartment which they now occupy. See, I and my maidens have been weaving their figures into this piece of tapestry."

She pointed to the web of beautifully woven cloth in the loom. Circe and the four nymphs must have been very diligently at work since the arrival of the mariners, for a great many yards of tapestry had now been wrought. In this new part Odysseus saw his two-and-twenty friends represented as sitting on cushioned and canopied thrones, greedily devouring dainties, and quaffing deep draughts of wine. The work had not yet gone any farther. Oh no, indeed! The enchantress was far too cunning to let Odysseus see the mischief which her magic arts had since brought upon the gormandizers.

"As for yourself, valiant sir," said Circe, "judging by the dignity of your aspect, I take you to be nothing less than a king. Deign to follow me, and you shall be treated as befits your rank."

So Odysseus followed her into the saloon, where his two-and-twenty comrades had devoured the banquet which ended so disastrously for themselves. But all this while he had held the snow-white flower in his hand, and had constantly smelt of it while Circe was speaking; and as he crossed the threshold of the saloon, he took good care to inhale several long and deep snuffs of its fragrance. Instead of two-and-twenty thrones, which had before been ranged around the wall, there was now only a single throne in the centre of the apartment. But this was surely the most magnificent seat that ever a king or an emperor reposed himself upon, all made of chased gold, studded with precious stones, with a cushion that looked like a soft heap of living roses, and overhung by a canopy of sunlight, which Circe knew how to weave into drapery. The enchantress took Odysseus by the hand, and made him sit down upon this dazzling throne. Then, clapping her hands, she summoned the chief butler.

"Bring hither," said she, "the goblet that is set apart for kings to drink out of. And fill it with the same delicious wine which my royal brother, King Æetes, praised so highly when he last visited me with my fair daughter Medea. That good and amiable child! Were she now here, it would delight her to see me offering this wine to my honoured guest."

But Odysseus, while the butler was gone for the wine, held the snow-white flower to his nose.

"Is it a wholesome wine?" he asked.

At this the four maidens tittered; whereupon the enchantress looked round at them with an aspect of severity.

"It is the wholesomest juice that ever was squeezed out of the grape," said she; "for instead of disguising a man, as other liquor is apt to do, it brings him to his true self, and shows him as he ought to be."

The chief butler liked nothing better than to see people turned into swine, or making any kind of a beast of themselves; so he made haste to bring the royal goblet, filled with a liquid as bright as gold, and which kept sparkling upward, and throwing a sunny spray over the brim. But, delightful as the wine looked, it was mingled with the most potent enchantments that Circe knew how to concoct. For every drop of the pure grape-juice there were two drops of the pure mischief; and the danger of the thing was that the mischief made it taste all the better. The mere smell of the bubbles which effervesced at the brim was enough to turn a man's beard into pig's bristles, or make a lion's claws grow out of his fingers, or a fox's brush behind him.

"Drink, my noble guest," said Circe, smiling as she presented him with the goblet. "You will find in this draught a solace for all your troubles."

King Odysseus took the goblet with his right hand, while with his left he held the snow-white flower to his nostrils and drew in so long a breath that his lungs were quite filled with its pure and simple fragrance. Then, drinking off all the wine, he looked the enchantress calmly in the face.

"Wretch," cried Circe, giving him a smart stroke with her wand, "how dare you keep your human shape a moment longer? Take the form of the brute whom you most resemble. If a hog, go join your fellow-swine in the sty; if a lion, a wolf, a tiger, go howl with the wild beasts on the lawn; if a fox, go exercise your craft in stealing poultry. Thou hast quaffed off my wine, and canst be a man no longer."

But such was the virtue of the snow-white flower, instead of wallowing down from his throne in swinish shape, or taking any other brutal form, Odysseus looked even more manly and kingly than before. He gave the magic goblet a toss, and sent it clashing over the marble floor to the farthest end of the saloon. Then, drawing his sword, he seized the enchantress by her beautiful ringlets, and made a gesture as if he meant to strike off her head at one blow.

"Wicked Circe," cried he, in a terrible voice, "this sword shall put an end to thy enchantments. Thou shalt die, vile wretch, and do no more mischief in the world by tempting human beings into the vices which make beasts of them."

The tone and countenance of Odysseus were so awful, and his sword gleamed so brightly, and seemed to have so intolerably keen an edge, that Circe was almost killed by the mere fright, without waiting for a blow. The chief butler scrambled out of the saloon, picking up the golden goblet as he went; and the enchantress and the four maidens fell on their knees, wringing their hands and screaming for mercy.

"Spare me!" cried Circe, "spare me, royal and wise Odysseus. For now I know that thou art he of whom Quicksilver forewarned me, the most prudent of mortals, against whom no enchantments can prevail. Thou only couldst have conquered Circe. Spare me, wisest of men. I will show thee true hospitality, and even give myself to be thy slave, and this magnificent palace to be henceforth thy home."

Odysseus would not be pacified until Circe had taken a solemn oath to change back his companions, and as many others as he should direct, from their present forms of beast or bird into their former shapes of men.

"On these conditions," said he, in a solemn tone of voice, "I consent to spare your life. Otherwise you must die upon the spot."

With a drawn sword hanging over her, the enchantress would readily have consented to do as much good as she had hitherto done mischief, however little she might like such employment. She therefore led Odysseus out of the back entrance of the palace, and showed him the swine in their sty.

"These must certainly be my comrades," said Odysseus; "I recognize their dispositions. They are hardly worth the trouble of changing them into the human form again. Nevertheless, we will have it done, lest their bad example should corrupt the other hogs. Let them take their original shapes, therefore, Dame Circe, if your skill is equal to the task. It will require greater magic, I trow, than it did to make swine of them."

So Circe waved her wand again, and repeated a few magic words, at the sound of which the two-and-twenty hogs pricked up their pendulous ears. It was a wonder to behold how their snouts grew shorter and shorter, and their mouths (which they seemed to be sorry for, because they could not gobble so expeditiously) smaller and smaller, and how one and another began to stand upon his hindlegs, and scratch his nose with his fore trotters. At first the spectators hardly knew whether to call them hogs or men, but by and by they came to the conclusion that they rather resembled the latter. Finally, there stood the twenty-two comrades of Odysseus, looking pretty much the same as when they left the vessel.

To say the truth, there was a suspicious kind of a grunt in their voices, and for a long time afterwards they spoke gruffly, and were apt to set up a squeal.

"It must depend on your own future behaviour," added Odysseus, "whether you do not find your way back to the sty."

At this moment the note of a bird sounded from the branch of a neighbouring tree.

"Peep, peep, pe—wee—ep!"

It was the purple bird, who all this while had been sitting over their heads, watching what was going forward, and hoping that Odysseus would remember how he had done his utmost to keep him and his followers out of harm's way. Odysseus ordered Circe instantly to make a king of this good little fowl, and leave him exactly as she found him. Hardly were the words spoken, and before the bird had time to utter another "Pe—weep", King Picus leaped down from the bough of the tree, as majestic a sovereign as any in the world, dressed in a long purple robe and gorgeous yellow stockings, with a splendidly wrought collar about his neck, and a golden crown upon his head. He and King Odysseus exchanged with one another the courtesies which belonged to their elevated rank. But from that time forth King Picus was no longer proud of his crown and his trappings of royalty, nor of the fact of his being a king: he felt himself merely the upper servant of his people, and that it must be his lifelong labour to make them better and happier.

As for the lions, tigers, and wolves (though Circe would have restored them to their former shapes at his slightest word), Odysseus thought it advisable that they should remain as they now were and thus give warning of their cruel dispositions, instead of going about under the guise of men, and pretending to human sympathies, while their hearts had the bloodthirstiness of wild beasts. So he let them howl as much as they liked, but never troubled his head about them. And when everything was settled according to his pleasure, he sent to summon the remainder of his comrades, whom he had left at the seashore. These being arrived, with the prudent Eurylochus at their head, they all made themselves comfortable in Circe's enchanted palace until quite rested and refreshed from the toils and hardships of their voyage.

PHAETHON

Phaethon's story is proof that divine parentage is not always a boon. Phaethon's father was the god Helios, who was born during the titan generation. Each morning, Helios boarded his chariot and was driven through the sky by flying horses, the sun drawn behind them. With a name that meant 'radiance', one might expect Phaethon to take after his father. However, the children of gods and goddesses did not always share in their parents' gifts. Yet Phaethon was determined to have his divine lineage proven and so pleaded with his father to let him ride the chariot. Perhaps the young man hoped to be the next Heracles or Orpheus, who took after their own sires Zeus and Apollo in turn. Or maybe he was just a young man trying to belong. Whatever his reasons, his request was foolhardy, and the results are clear when you read the following story.

Phaethon was the child of Helios, the sun-god. One could see the glint of the sun's rays in his bright yellow hair, and feel its warmth in the flash of his eyes. He was so full of life and energy that it was a pleasure to watch him. When he was playing with the other boys in the village, if they threw stones, it was Phaethon who could throw the farthest; if they ran races, Phaethon always reached the goal first; and it was the same in all their other sports.

Although these boys could not beat Phaethon in their games, they could say rude things to him, and one day, because they wished to get the better of him in some way, they all met him with a chorus of taunts and sneering words. Among other things, they said that he was not the child of Helios, and this hurt Phaethon very much, for he had always thought it a glorious thing to feel that the god of the great shining sun was his father.

The next morning, as he lay under a tree, gazing steadfastly at the sun, he thought he could see the sun-god, Helios, driving his golden chariot across the sky. "What a fine thing it would be," he said to himself, "if I, boy as I am, could drive that splendid chariot! Then the boys would believe that I am really the child of the sun-god."

The thought had no sooner entered his head than he set out to go to the country where the sun rises. It was a long journey, but at last he saw the golden palace of the sun-god; and then, as he came nearer, he saw Helios himself, sitting on a throne with a crown on his head, while the Hours and the Days stood around him ready to do his bidding. The crown that Helios wore was the most wonderful crown that was ever seen; it was set thick with precious stones of the most dazzling kind; in fact, these stones were so bright that they cast rays of light all around, and whoever looked at them long was sure to be almost blinded.

Even Phaethon's eyes could not long bear the brightness of the crown, so he stood well back from it and told Helios who he was and what the boys had said. Then he asked if there were not some way by which his playmates could be made to believe that he was really the child of the Sun.

Helios took off his crown, so that Phaethon could come nearer, and then he promised to grant any wish that the boy should make. This was a great favor, and Phaethon would not have received it if he had not been a true child of the Sun.

Phaethon clapped his hands in triumph; for he thought that now he might have his wish. The Hours were already bringing out the golden chariot of the Sun, and it seemed almost as bright as the crown of Helios. Phaethon asked instantly if he might not drive this chariot for one day.

Helios was troubled at hearing such a wish as this, but he had promised, and the gods could not break their promises; accordingly, when the Hours brought out the horses, and made everything ready, he was obliged to let Phaethon take the reins.

The horses of the Sun were powerful animals, as fiery in their temper as any creature that ever lived, even in those days of fire-breathing bulls and dragons. They seemed to be made of fire inside, and they reared and plunged and champed their bits in a way that would have thoroughly frightened most boys. But Phaethon, remembering that he was a child of the Sun, gladly took his place in the chariot.

The four horses started off at a gallop, and Phaethon was so light that the chariot was tossed back and forth as if it had been empty. The horses were frightened at once. They left the right path round the world, and began to run wildly, swerving first one way and then another.

Phaethon saw now, when it was too late, that he was too young to drive such horses. They grew more and more excited, and sparks of fire began to fly from their nostrils. The chariot, too, as it was carried faster and faster through space, began to grow brighter and hotter.

As the horses and chariot came close to the earth, mountain tops took fire and began to smoke. They came closer yet, rivers were dried up, and many, many miles of forest-land and green meadows were scorched and became like a desert. In some countries, too, the heat was so great that the people of those countries were turned to a dark color. It looked as if the whole world might be burned up.

By this time Phaethon was terrified, indeed, for his own hair was on fire. But he did not know what to do.

Zeus, looking down from Mount Olympus, saw that the world was in great danger. Then suddenly came a terrible clap of thunder, and Phaethon fell from the chariot, down, straight down, like a falling star, into the broad river Eridanus.

And so poor Phaethon, though a true child of the Sun, failed in trying to drive his father's fiery chariot. Perhaps he would never have attempted so daring a deed, had it not been for the unkind taunts of his playfellows. There are some things which even the children of the Sun cannot do.

His sisters, the Heliades, wept for him on the banks of the Eridanus, till at last they were changed into larch trees; and their tears, continuing to fall into the water from the branches of the trees, became drops of clear amber.

PYGMALION AND GALATEA

The myth of Pygmalion and Galatea must be one of the strangest 'love stories' of ancient Greek myth, if you can even call it that. This is the tale of a man so unimpressed with what humanity has to offer that he makes for himself the perfect woman out of stone. When his inanimate lover proves still not enough, however, he longs for Aphrodite to breathe life into her marble chest. What is strange is not Pygmalion's disinterest in others, or his persistent desire for love, but the way in which he goes about crafting for himself the perfect woman when no one else will do. Galatea seemingly exists purely for her sculptor's gratification, so it is no wonder that even adaptations of this myth have turned away from her rocky origins: *My Fair Lady* springs to mind. Yet while unpalatable to some, it is an equally fascinating tale, as Josephine Preston Peabody proves.

The island of Cyprus was dear to the heart of Aphrodite. There her temples were kept with honor, and there, some say, she watched with the Loves and Graces over the long enchanted sleep of Adonis. This youth, a hunter whom she had dearly loved, had died of a wound from the tusk of a wild boar; but the bitter grief of Aphrodite had won over even the powers of Hades. For six months of every year, Adonis had to live as a Shade in the world of the dead, but for the rest of the time he was free to breathe the upper air. Here in Cyprus the people came to worship him as a god, for the sake of Aphrodite who loved him; and here, if any called upon her, she was like to listen.

Now there once lived in Cyprus a young sculptor, Pygmalion by name, who thought nothing on earth so beautiful as the white marble folk that live without faults and never grow old. Indeed, he said that he would never marry a mortal woman, and people began to think that his daily life among marble creatures was hardening his heart altogether.

But it chanced that Pygmalion fell to work upon an ivory statue of a maiden, so lovely that it must have moved to envy every breathing creature that came to look upon it. With a happy heart the sculptor wrought day by day, giving it all the beauty of his dreams, until, when the work was completed, he felt powerless to leave it. He was bound to it by the tie of his highest aspiration, his most perfect ideal, his most patient work.

Day after day the ivory maiden looked down at him silently, and he looked back at her until he felt that he loved her more than anything else in the world. He thought of her no longer as a statue, but as the dear companion of his life; and the whim grew upon him like an enchantment. He named her Galatea, and arrayed her like a princess; he hung jewels about her neck, and made all his home beautiful and fit for such a presence.

Now the festival of Aphrodite was at hand, and Pygmalion, like all who loved Beauty, joined the worshippers. In the temple victims were offered, solemn rites were held, and votaries from many lands came to pray the favor of the goddess. At length Pygmalion himself approached the altar and made his prayer.

"Goddess," he said, "who hast vouchsafed to me this gift of beauty, give me a perfect love, likewise, and let me have for bride, one like my ivory maiden." And Aphrodite heard.

Home to his house of dreams went the sculptor, loath to be parted for a day from his statue, Galatea. There she stood, looking down upon him silently, and he looked back at her. Surely the sunset had shed a flush of life upon her whiteness.

He drew near in wonder and delight, and felt, instead of the chill air that was wont to wake him out of his spell, a gentle warmth around her, like the breath of a plant. He touched her hand, and it yielded like the hand of one living! Doubting his senses, yet fearing to reassure himself, Pygmalion kissed the statue.

In an instant the maiden's face bloomed like a waking rose, her hair shone golden as returning sunlight; she lifted her ivory eyelids and smiled at him. The statue herself had awakened, and she stepped down from the pedestal, into the arms of her creator, alive!

There was a dream that came true.

CEYX AND HALCYONE

If it was not clear by now, let us conclude this collection with one final reminder to respect the ancient Greek gods and goddesses, lest your fate mirror that of Ceyx and Halcyone. Ceyx was the semi-divine king of Trachis and Halcyone was the daughter of the king of Aeolia. The two married and lived such blissful lives together that they considered themselves akin to Zeus and Hera, the king and queen of Olympus. To compare oneself to the gods and goddesses in ancient Greek myth was tantamount to sacrilege, and the gods did not refrain from punishing those who did. On one final note, however, it is worth remembering that once lost, the approval of ancient Greek deities can yet be regained. Whether this is what happened to Halcyone and Ceyx can only be learned by reading on.

"St. Martin's summer, halcyon days."
King Henry VI, i. 2, 131.

"Halcyon days"—how often is the expression made use of, how seldom do its users realise from whence they have borrowed it.

"These were halcyon days," says the old man, and his memory wanders back to a time when for him

"All the world is young, lad,
And all the trees are green;
And every goose a swan, lad,
And every lass a queen."

Yet the story of Halcyone is one best to be understood by the heavy-hearted woman who wanders along the bleak sea beach and strains her weary eyes for the brown sail of the fishing-boat that will never more return.

Over the kingdom of Thessaly, in the days of long ago, there reigned a king whose name was

Ceyx, son of Hesperus, the Day Star, and almost as radiant in grace and beauty as was his father. His wife was the fair Halcyone, daughter of Æolus, ruler of the winds, and most perfectly did this king and queen love one another. Their happiness was unmarred until there came a day when Ceyx had to mourn for the loss of a brother. Following close on the heels of this disaster came direful prodigies which led Ceyx to fear that in some way he must have incurred the hostility of the gods. To him there was no way in which to discover wherein lay his fault, and to make atonement for it, but by going to consult the oracle of Apollo at Claros, in Ionia. When he told Halcyone what he must do, she knew well that she must not try to turn him from his solemn purpose, yet there hung over her heart a black shadow of fear and of evil foreboding that no loving words of assurance could drive away. Most piteously she begged him to take her with him, but the king knew too well the dangers of the treacherous Ægean Sea to risk on it the life of the woman that he loved so well.

"I promise," he said, "by the rays of my Father the Day Star, that if fate permits I will return before the moon shall have twice rounded her orb."

Down by the shore the sailors of King Ceyx awaited his coming, and when with passionately tender love he and Halcyone had taken farewell of each other, the rowers sat down on the benches and dipped their long oars into the water.

With rhythmic swing they drove the great ship over the grey sea, while Ceyx stood on deck and gazed back at his wife until his eyes could no longer distinguish her from the rocks on the shore, nor could she any longer see the white sails of the ship as it crested the restless waves. Heavier still was her heart when she turned away from the shore, and yet more heavy it grew as the day wore on and dark night descended. For the air was full of the clamorous wailings of the fierce winds whose joy it is to lash the waves into rage and to strew with dead men and broken timber the angry, surf-beaten shore.

"My King," she sighed to herself. "My King! my Own!" And through the weary hours she prayed to the gods to bring him safely back to her, and many times she offered fragrant incense to Hera, protectress of women, that she might have pity on a woman whose husband and true lover was out in the storm, a plaything for ruthless winds and waves.

A helpless plaything was the king of Thessaly. Long ere the dim evening light had made of the shore of his own land a faint, grey line, the white-maned horses of Poseidon, king of the seas, began to rear their heads, and as night fell, a black curtain, blotting out every landmark, and all home-like things, the East Wind rushed across the Ægean Sea, smiting the sea-horses into madness, seizing the sails with cruel grasp and casting them in tatters before it, snapping the mast as though it were but a dry reed by the river. Before so mighty a tempest no oars could be of any avail, and for a little time only the winds and waves gambolled like a half-sated wolf-pack over their helpless prey. With hungry roar the great weight of black water stove in the deck and swept the sailors out of the ship to choke them in its icy depths; and ever it would lift the wounded thing high up on its foaming white crests, as though to toss it to the dark sky, and ever again would suck it down into the blackness, while the shrieking winds drove it onward with howling taunts and mocking laughter. While life stayed in him, Ceyx thought only of Halcyone. He had no fear, only the fear of the grief his death must bring to her who loved him as he loved her, his peerless queen, his Halcyone. His prayers to the gods were prayers for her. For himself he asked one thing only—that the waves might bear his body to her sight, so that her gentle hands might lay him in his tomb. With shout of triumph that they had slain a king, winds and waves seized him even as he prayed, and the Day Star that was hidden behind the black pall of the sky knew that his son, a brave king and a faithful lover, had gone down to the Shades.

When Dawn, the rosy-fingered, had come to Thessaly, Halcyone, white-faced and tired-eyed, anxiously watched the sea, that still was tossing in half-savage mood. Eagerly she gazed at the place where last the white sail had been seen. Was it not possible that Ceyx, having weathered the gale, might for the present have foregone his voyage to Ionia, and was returning to her to bring peace to her heart? But the sea-beach was strewn with wrack and the winds still blew bits of tattered surf along the shore, and for her there was only the heavy labour of waiting, of waiting and of watching for the ship that never came. The incense from her altars blew out, in heavy sweetness, to meet the bitter-sweet tang of the seaweed that was carried in by the tide, for Halcyone prayed on, fearful, yet hoping that her prayers might still keep safe her man—her king—her lover. She busied herself in laying out the garments he would wear on his return, and in choosing the clothes in which she might be fairest in his eyes. This robe, as blue as the sky in spring—silver-bordered, as the sea in kind mood is bordered with a feathery silver fringe.

She could recall just how Ceyx looked when first he saw her wear it. She could hear his very tones as he told her that of all queens she was the peeress, of all women the most beautiful, of all wives the most dear. Almost she forgot the horrors of the night, so certain did it seem that his dear voice must soon again tell her the words that have been love's litany since ever time began.

In the ears of Hera those petitions for him whose dead body was even then being tossed hither and thither by the restless waves, his murderers, came at last to be more than even she could bear. She gave command to her handmaiden Iris to go to the palace of Somnus, god of Sleep and brother of Death, and to bid him send to Halcyone a vision, in the form of Ceyx, to tell her that all her weary waiting was in vain.

In a valley among the black Cimmerian mountains, the death-god Somnus had his abode. In her rainbow-hued robes, Iris darted through the sky at her mistress's bidding, tingeing, as she sped through them, the clouds that she passed. It was a silent valley that she reached at last. Here the sun never came, nor was there ever any sound to break the silence. From the ground the noiseless grey clouds, whose work it is to hide the sun and moon, rose softly and rolled away up to the mountain tops and down to the lowest valleys, to work the will of the gods. All around the cave lurked the long dark shadows that bring fear to the heart of children, and that, at nightfall, hasten the steps of the timid wayfarer. No noise was there, but from far down the valley there came a murmur so faint and so infinitely soothing that it was less a sound than of a lullaby remembered in dreams. For past the valley of Sleep flow the waters of Lethe, the river of Forgetfulness, close up to the door of the cave where dwelt the twin-brothers, Sleep and Death, blood-red poppies grew, and at the door itself stood shadowy forms, their fingers on their lips, enjoining silence on all those who would enter in, amaranth-crowned, and softly waving sheaves of poppies that bring dreams from which there is no awakening. There was there no gate with hinges to creak or bars to clang, and into the stilly darkness Iris walked unhindered. From outer cave to inner cave she went, and each cave she left behind was less dark than the one that she entered. In the innermost room of all, on an ebony couch draped with sable curtains, the god of sleep lay drowsing. His garments were black, strewn with golden stars. A wreath of half-opened poppies crowned his sleepy head, and he leaned on the strong shoulder of Morpheus, his favourite son. All round his bed hovered pleasant dreams, gently stooping over him to whisper their messages, like a field of wheat swayed by the breeze, or willows that bow their silver heads and murmur to each other the secrets that no one ever knows. Brushing the idle dreams aside, as a ray of sunshine brushes away the grey wisps of mist that hang to the hillside, Iris walked up to the couch where Somnus lay. The light from her rainbow-hued robe lit up the darkness of the cave, yet Somnus lazily only half-opened his eyes, moved his head so that it rested more easily, and in a sleepy voice asked of her what might be her errand. "Somnus," she said, "gentlest of gods, tranquilliser of minds and soother of careworn hearts, Hera sends you her commands that you despatch a dream to Halcyone in the city of Trachine, representing her lost husband and all the events of the wreck."

Her message delivered, Iris hastened away, for it seemed to her that already her eyelids grew heavy, and that there were creeping upon her limbs, throwing silver dust in her eyes, lulling into peaceful slumber her mind, those sprites born of the blood-red poppies that bring to weary mortals rest and sweet forgetfulness.

Only rousing himself sufficiently to give his orders, Somnus entrusted to Morpheus the task imposed upon him by Hera, and then, with a yawn, turned over on his downy pillow, and gave himself up to exquisite slumber.

When he had winged his way to Trachine, Morpheus took upon himself the form of Ceyx and sought the room where Halcyone slept. She had watched the far horizon many hours that day. For many an hour had she vainly burned incense to the gods. Tired in heart and soul, in body and in mind, she laid herself down on her couch at last, hoping for the gift of sleep. Not long had she slept, in the dead-still sleep that weariness and a stricken heart bring with them, when Morpheus came and stood by her side. He was only a dream, yet his face was the face of Ceyx. Not the radiant, beautiful son of the Day Star was the Ceyx who stood by her now and gazed on her with piteous, pitying dead eyes. His clothing dripped sea-water; in his hair was tangled the weed of the sea, uprooted by the storm. Pale, pale was his face, and his white hands gripped the stones and sand that had failed him in his dying agony.

Halcyone whimpered in her sleep as she looked on him, and Morpheus stooped over her and spoke the word that he had been told to say.

"I am thy husband, Ceyx, Halcyone. No more do prayers and the blue-curling smoke of incense avail me. Dead am I, slain by the storm and the waves. On my dead, white face the skies look down and the restless sea tosses my chill body that still seeks thee, seeking a haven in thy dear arms, seeking rest on thy warm, loving heart."

With a cry Halcyone started up, but Morpheus had fled, and there were no wet footprints nor drops of sea-water on the floor, marking, as she had hoped, the way that her lord had taken. Not again did Sleep visit her that night.

A grey, cold morning dawned and found her on the seashore. As ever, her eyes sought the far horizon, but no white sail, a messenger of hope, was there to greet her. Yet surely she saw something—a black speck, like a ship driven on by the long oars of mariners who knew well the path to home through the watery ways. From far away in the grey it hasted towards her, and then there came to Halcyone the knowledge that no ship was this thing, but a lifeless body, swept onwards by the hurrying waves. Nearer and nearer it came, until at length she could recognise the form of this flotsam and jetsam of the sea. With heart that broke as she uttered the words, she stretched out her arms and cried aloud: "O Ceyx! my Beloved! is it thus that thou returnest to me?"

To break the fierce assaults of sea and of storm

there had been built out from the shore a mole, and on to this barrier leapt the distraught Halcyone. She ran along it, and when the dead, white body of the man she loved was still out of reach, she prayed her last prayer—a wordless prayer of anguish to the gods.

"Only let me get near him," she breathed. "Grant only that I nestle close against his dear breast. Let me show him that, living or dead, I am his, and he mine forever."

And to Halcyone a great miracle was then vouchsafed, for from out of her snowy shoulders grew snow-white pinions, and with them she skimmed over the waves until she reached the rigid body of Ceyx, drifting, a helpless burden for the conquering waves, in with the swift-flowing tide. As she flew, she uttered cries of love and of longing, but only strange raucous cries came from the throat that had once only made music. And when she reached the body of Ceyx and would fain have kissed his marble lips, Halcyone found that no longer were her own lips like the petals of a fair red rose warmed by the sun. For the gods had heard her prayer, and her horny beak seemed to the watchers on the shore to be fiercely tearing at the face of him who had been king of Thessaly.

Yet the gods were not merciless—or, perhaps,

the love of Halcyone was an all-conquering love. For as the soul of Halcyone had passed into the body of a white-winged sea-bird, so also passed the soul of her husband the king. And for evermore Halcyone and her mate, known as the Halcyon birds, defied the storm and tempest, and proudly breasted, side by side, the angriest waves of the raging seas.

To them, too, did the gods grant a boon: that, for seven days before the shortest day of the year, and for seven days after it, there should reign over the sea a great calm in which Halcyone, in her floating nest, should hatch her young. And to those days of calm and sunshine, the name of the Halcyon Days was given.

And still, as a storm approaches, the white-winged birds come flying inland with shrill cries of warning to the mariners whose ships they pass in their flight.

"Ceyx!" they cry. "Remember Ceyx!"

And hastily the fishermen fill their sails, and the smacks drive homeward to the haven where the blue smoke curls upwards from the chimneys of their homesteads, and where the red poppies are nodding sleepily amongst the yellow corn.

Glossary

Admetus	king of Pherae
Alcestis	queen of Pherae
Apollo	god of music and healing
Ares	god of war
Argonauts	the crew of a ship called the *Argo*
Artemis	goddess of the hunt
Atalanta	princess of Arcadia and renowned huntress
Athene/Athena	goddess of wisdom and war
Bellerophon	the Greek hero who tamed Pegasus
Cadmus	founder of Thebes
Calliope	the muse of epic poetry
Centaurs	men who were half human, half horse
Cerberus	the three-headed dog that guards the underworld
Ceyx	king of Trachis and husband of Halcyone
Circe	goddess and witch
Cyclopes	one-eyed giants
Danae	mother of Perseus
Daedalus	legendary inventor

Demeter	goddess of the harvest
Dionysus	god of wine
Eros	god of love
Europa	princess kidnapped by Zeus
Eurydice	wife of Orpheus
Furies	goddesses of vengeance
Galatea	sculpture brought to life by Aphrodite
Hades	god of the underworld
Halcyone	queen of Trachis and wife of Ceyx
Helen	the most beautiful woman on earth
Helios	titan and god of the sun
Hera	goddess of marriage
Heracles	hero and half-mortal son of Zeus
Hermes	the messenger god
Hephaestus	god of craftsmanship
Hestia	goddess of the hearth
Icarus	son of Daedalus
Jason	captain of the *Argo*
Medusa	a snake-headed gorgon who turns men to stone
Medea	princess of Colchis and witch
Meleager	prince of Calydon
Menelaus	king of Sparta and husband of Helen

Midas	king who could turn things to gold with only his touch
Minos	king of Crete
Morpheus	god of dreams
Nereids	minor sea deities
Nymphs	minor nature deities
Odysseus	king of Ithaca
Olympian	third and final generation of Gods, ruled by Zeus
Olympus	the mountain on which the gods and goddesses resided
Orpheus	legendary musician
Pan	god of the wild
Paris	prince of Troy
Pegasus	a flying horse
Persephone	goddess of spring and queen of the underworld
Phaethon	son of Helios
Pythia	priestess of Apollo and prophet
Pygmalion	legendary sculptor
Poseidon	god of the sea
Tartarus	the deepest part of the Underworld
Titans	the second generation of gods
Uranus	god of the sky
Zeus	god of lightning and king of Olympus

MACMILLAN COLLECTOR'S LIBRARY

**Own the world's great works of literature in
one beautiful collectible library**

Designed and curated to appeal to book lovers everywhere,
Macmillan Collector's Library editions are small enough to
travel with you and striking enough to take pride of place
on your bookshelf. These much-loved literary classics
also make the perfect gift.

Beautifully produced with gilt edges, a ribbon marker,
bespoke illustrated cover and real cloth binding, every
Macmillan Collector's Library hardback adheres to the
same high production values.

Discover something new or cherish your favourite
stories with this elegant collection.

**Macmillan Collector's Library:
own, collect, and treasure**

Discover the full range at
macmillancollectorslibrary.com